T0150943

I Know Where I'm Going

Fran Carlen

ADVENTURES IN POETRY

Some of these poems appeared
in the following publications:
Combo, Fence, The Germ,
Great American Prose Poems:
From Poe to the Present, Hanging Loose,
Insurance, Paragraph, and *Sal Mimeo*

Thanks to Dave Johnson and Drew Gardner
for their help with the drumming nomenclature.

Cover watercolor by Win Knowlton
Book design by *typeslowly*
Printed in Canada

Adventures in Poetry titles are distributed
through Zephyr Press by
Consortium Book Sales and Distribution
www.cbsd.com
&
SPD: Small Press Distribution
www.spdbooks.org

ISBN 0-9706250-6-5

9 8 7 6 5 4 3 2 FIRST PRINTING IN 2003

ADVENTURES IN POETRY

NEW YORK   BOSTON

WWW.ADVENTURESINPOETRY.COM

CONTENTS

I Know Where I'm Going

SWEET RELIEF

I WAS WATCHING the game with a certain sang-froid. It was the same game as the many I'd played since I was a petite fille— seventh game of the World Series. A mood of auberge surrender in the dugout.

Robert Merrill sang "September Song." Libation bearers in the bleachers. Just above the press box a flock of impious bathers waved their pennants. Vendors hawked polenta, egg-anchovy canapés and pill-cups of Stoli. Would it be my last game before I departed for Chalon-sur-Saône to study puff pastry? I was out of the rotation again. Veiled allusions to a trade had hung in the pre-post-season air. What had I done besides bake and play ball? A smattering of magic. Some card tricks, sleights of hand. Dabbled in escapism—I could break out of chains and handcuffs from a trunk under water, but where was the future in that? Back in March, a M. Godard had come to Vero Beach to reassure us that if baseball didn't work out, there'd be promising careers galore in library science.

"Du bist der Mann," he uttered as I sprung to my feet. Everyone knew Mabüse was maestro of the unpredictable. "But. . . ." One withered hand on my shoulder. "Crossroads," whispered Johnson as he trudged from the mound. But he always said that. I'd left his room at a quarter past ten. He was curled up in a fetal twist. Mabüse'd taken away his Tele, his Strat, his ES 345, his Shortneck, his Firebird, his National, his dobro, and his comb. We watched him melt and fizzle, from staff ace to shell, shadow, zombie.

The batter limped to the plate, lame as a crooked dray. Wagged the bat to and fro like a clumsy jug, and anxiously pawed the brim of his cap. I felt I knew everything about him—not just his stats but the contents of his double-door fridge, the names of the kids he hadn't had. He batted left was all that mattered. The low swoon of a curve that swerved languidly like an old pro working the lounge suddenly broke toward Poland before the definitive thwunk in the mitt.

The gaze of my swaddled batterymate, Zambinella. Our secret subsemiotic code. Whenever he shrugged sultrily and/or my hand absently grazed my left breast, I would throw down and out. If he sighed resignedly or my eyes narrowed like Catherine on the wheel, it was the slider. Heady rush of primordial brute force. Ponder the instability of miracles, the deadlines of auguries. Fingers clenched damp twine triumph. I loosened my grip.

My eye caught the unfurling banner behind the backstop: DEEP SIX THE PREHENSILES. They'd forgotten to hyphenate again. Globoid shot high and outside. Ball. Mabüse applied chapstick with mad-dog pragmatism, the signal for me to bean. My whistling-tea-kettle two-seam blazer. Primitive Blutfest. Crack of the bat, frozen rope through short, runner to second, no tag. I glanced around to see first and short in wicked kinship, looked to Mabüse, deadpanning the pitchout. Runner fairly nailed to the bag. Behind second a body. I trot out to the edge of the infield. The ump follows like a mutt. Lying face down, dressed in hobo jacket, short pants, little workboots, a newsboy cap. I kick it over on its back—a bug in boy's clothes. I look to the ump to help me carry it off. He points fiercely to the mound.

Mabüse stands with his arms folded, grinning at nothing. I return to the mound and face the DH. Stinging blast of verité. We came up through the minors together. He didn't have the moustache then. My screwball, side-armed slider, the let's-get-lost curve, ain't-nobody's-business knuckler, and good-morning-heartache sinker—he knew them all. Z. was giving me more signs than Saussure, but I walk the batter meekly on four.

I glance back at the bug but it's gone! I do a little torque and catch the runner stealing third. But where's the bug? I scour the field, give the grandstands the once-over. Time has disappeared from the big digital clock, innings and score missing. I take a deep breath, roll my shoulders, go into the wind-up, and there it is, sitting propped up next to Mabüse in the dugout. I hate creepy crawlers! The ump calls a balk. What's it doing here at my big moment! "Damn vermin," I mutter. The ump thinks I mean him. Fans hurl their batteries onto the field. Mabüse intervenes and peace is restored.

I look back up at the board. Stats have returned. No more bug in the dugout. Perhaps it was just a case of nerves. But who knows where it'll pop up next? One more out to go. My fingers shiver as I fling the floater. The bat cracks, the ball flies up. The insect crawls over the mound. I stick up my glove and squeeze my eyes shut. It plops in the pocket. The crowd goes schooly.

SLIDE

HE TOLD HER himself this is scary when she told him she liked his trombone playing. She said she was scared too which was true but she was also pleased. She could hear the fear in his voice, the suggestion of being together, also the idea of seeing each other, or the Italian restaurant he talked about taking her to.

The voice she heard was smug but also friendly. It reminded her of crime novels. Tell me which side you want the shiner on. Full of deliberate pauses. Get out of the water. I'm going to be like this for a while. You're making me like you. She liked the way voices sounded, the edgy trembling of telling, sudden shyness, forgetting words, saying the wrong ones, when she said how she and/or it all depended upon . . . the anxiety in his voice telling her he had to call his sister.

His trombone voice was somber. It came from a dormitory room with an alarm clock and dice. In the bell she heard prowlers, the morning papers. It made her think of her own recurrent apocalypse dream—apothecary-bottle air, shadow in the shape of a hand, horizon line where the storm or war advances. Or was this just normal woe, the monotone of trombone?

Still she knew he knew something. An eclipse passed between the sun and us the second he was born. No one remembered when that was, no record of it. He said that he was born in Newark and he should know. She wondered how he knew how things came to nothing. She could see he knew that look that goes back behind the space of waiting.

She knew it frightened him to tell her what he knew. Instead he told her the categories of clouds, hands, birdfeet, things she knew already. She wanted to get back to sleep, the arrangement of it, before sounds and pauses. She was also pretty sure of the future.

DO YOU KNOW THE WAY TO NIKETOWN?

MOVING TOWARD THE blowdryers, clasping one and waving it vacantly around my head, with less finesse than the others, styling inasmuch as a cyclone styles a subdivision. Still, I had my products. Mother had spoken of *upkeep*. She reminded me how haggard I would become. The bombshell on my left is making synchronous strokes with hotcomb and hairspray. The sinister hiss is aimed at me.

Off to the hospital to visit a new mother. The new father in the Hawaiian shirt is making a case for the name Odile. The other woman in the room is removed on a gurney. The odor of fresh corpse mingles with ammonia and dead flowers. I have nothing against hospitals. But you could open a window before the war. I wouldn't eat a sandwich here if I had one.

So I escaped. The weather was mixed but rain was predicted. I walked weaving in and out of out-of-towners, dodging monsters milling on corners. I resolved to get where I was going, no matter where that was, but my mind outstripped my legs, humming all the chart-toppers, so I didn't see the FedEx truck running the red heading straight at me. Passing through me.

Tables were set up along the sidewalk. I wouldn't dream of sitting down at one. A man approached and asked me how to get to NikeTown. I gave him explicit directions, the precise number of blocks, landmarks to look out for, an alternate route. I took his map and traced the way with my forefinger, throwing in a few words of halting French, impersonal pronouns mostly. Starting again, I tripped over a seeing-eye dog; I have nothing against dogs but that dog needed a dog. But what could I say to the blind man—watch your dog? As I got up he poked me in the leg with his stick and moved on. I bolted underground.

I began to feel sorry for myself. That was a thing to do. I was lonely but I was poor as well, don't you see. If only I could find money, perhaps in the gutter, instead of having to go without supper, then I could purchase the tiniest tube of *crème contour des yeux aux pépins de raisin*. But that is none of your beeswax.

I thought of Marble Hill. A favorite game of mother's was to take me across the tracks just when the train was coming. Shrieking in chorus with the train whistle, we'd rush down the rubbish-strewn decline to the water's edge. Crews were making their afternoon rounds, eight pairs of oars slicing in one firm semi-circular swoop, coxswain hairpinned backwards. Oh to be on the gray water, in a simple sunfish, skull, kayak, even a canoe with one splintered oar, or a Huck-and-Jim raft, and my Ultra Lite Oil-Free Sunblock SPF 30 with anti-oxidant micellized vitamins A & E and Parsol 1789. But I can't even afford an inner tube.

I ascended the steps counting backwards, stopping at the top to sound out the Cyrillic signs in the shop windows, clambered back down to the other side of the tracks. At the bottom I realized I was parched. I spotted a vendor at the overpass and crawled back up the steps. He was clean-cut like a theologian. I handed him two crumpled singles. Two seltzers, I said. What *kind* of seltzer? the Slav inquired.

Plain, I replied, dva, pozhalsta. Two *plain* seltzers, he repeated emphatically. *Two plain seltzers*, I pronounced syllabically, adding slowly, *in a bag*. I grabbed the parcel and tore down the stairs.

The train pulled in. I sat down beside a woman. Her lipstick was all down her chin. Fishing through her logoed tote, she pulled out *Conflict Management*, a slick circular. I grabbed a seltzer and opened it. It exploded and showered over her. Blotting madly, she found another seat. I slid over to the window. Then I dozed off.

The sun was setting over Times Square. I walked west. Then I walked east. I had no wish to be anywhere near water. I looked around for hookers—runaway girls and their pimps leaning against Lincolns—but none could be found. Where were the porn shops and the peep shows? Placards touted "Prime Retail Units" and announced "The 42nd Street Development Project." A crane nested atop steel girders, scaffolding was everywhere, and birds sailed overhead. Had there been birds before?

I was determined to find a sex shop if I had to comb the town and the city. Swerving north on Eighth I spotted a XXX Video and ambled in. I needed answers. I made a short tour of the Amateur section then sat down on a stepstool in the corner and slept. The clerk woke me. Help you? he said. I reflected. Is this store for rent? Without the videos? But what would I do with an empty store? I want live action, nothing rehearsed, no premise, no plot, a privileged behind-the-scenes glimpse, with, if possible, archival footage and subtitles—a *documentary*. How could I make him understand? I wandered out and into the pharmacy next door.

Aisles of jars and bottles and in the back a case containing assorted habiliments. The light heavyweight behind the beauty counter was placing a narrow black coffer out of sight. What is it? I asked. Inside the box, swaddled in cotton, was a cross between a glass potato masher and a garden hoe, two curved tines attached to a racket handle with a black cord. Want to see how it works? He plugged it in, took my hand and touched the tips to my palm; little electric shocks made my hand twitch. To jump-start the follicles. When your hair falls out put it right on your scalp. He moved to demonstrate. I took an automatic hop back. I wasn't losing my hair. Still I was fascinated. The champ quoted a figure higher than my monthly lunch and supper rations combined.

I staggered out depleted and deprived. Then I remembered that I still had a seltzer. The taste was exquisite. I tilted my head back 90 degrees and caught a glimpse of money in the gutter. Much money. William McKinleys, Grover Clevelands, Salmon P. Chases and one Woodrow Wilson spilling from a sack. I strolled back into the store and picked up a basket. In it I put Cleopatra Placenta, Yacht Club Brilliantine, No Lye Relaxer, Pure Vitamin Growth Crème, Colonial Dámes Fade and NuNile Pomade, a pail of Wave Nouveau, a Miracle Stone, a Slumber Masque, a twelve-pack apiece of Bulls-Eye Tipping Caps with Needle and Dark Brown Invisible Hairnets French Style, Megamousse Therapy, Speed Bleach, Punky Hair & Body Glitter, some Slicky Blackener, Lipstick Fix, Silky Puffs, a Squizzer and a Crimper, Glow-in-the-Dark Emery Boards and Sand Castle Top Coat, Bürstenreninger, Barbershop Tonic, Handmade

French Rollers and Double-Prong Hideaway Pins, Toe Spacers, a Chamois Buffer-Pumice Paddle Duo, a Folding Lash Comb & Curler, Teasing and Detangling Combs, Beauty Gloves, three Temporary Tattoo Kits with cards, snakes and daggers, and an inch-square tortoise-shell barrette in the shape of an Airedale. It was night when I left with my purchases. I hadn't eaten lunch yet. Then I remembered something else. I headed south toward Flower Power to pick up the tiny tube.

THAT'S THE KIND OF HAIRPIN I AM

I HAD TO make my body rigid from the legs up to stop myself from falling down. The air was solid, I could hardly ram through it. I found myself in an orthopedic store. A mother was putting ratchets on her tot. Then, suddenly, I was in the library. I had a pebble in my shoe and my wristwatch said skip lunch, be mindful of the lost tribe who only ate when it rained.

I set out to prove three things. I had nothing against monarchs and would never live outside the city. Every day I did something I didn't want to. If I couldn't explain it I couldn't explain it. There were times when I meant it. Or else I stayed in bed and read, for there were no deadlines or office hours.

The sacred ditched in a sudden reading. My pants were full of passages, a drought of sentiment ending in quietude.

A plain view of austerity or a room with no furniture, the cigarette before and after confession. I was still a long way from knowing why. Even when I broke it down. My thoughts ran along pure strong vinyl grooves. I sold a scarabaeus rolled up in a ball, indolence and distraction by the seashore.

Riding in a car anything is possible. A woman or an arc, a bun, feet brushing against nothing, wind, rest assured, lassoed, or tycoons inscribed by careless swinging. I know the sun is soft in Sardinia.

My place was no place for mirrors or dollies. Not that I minded a thunderstorm or a dangerous fever but gaiety was lost on me. I'd chosen a simple mantle of ashen dread. Made to repose on Ritz Crackers, my reading comprehension was soon stunted, and my speech became a chowder of mixed-up modifiers and faulty nerbs. Maximize your potential—which meant my wrists and ankles. By the time I was bored of joints, I was considered unteachable. In grief I lit the match they'd given me to play with.

Only a spider could make me look up. I wanted to grow up to become an equation or a horse. I, who sometimes thought long and hard about fabric. Venturesome, a little glazed, grasping the slipcovers. At an early age I knew jewels would do. Practicing *pas des chats* or the short dance done by the millipede whose works include "The Eve of St. Agnes."

My body was an amnesiac passing through glass. Flabbergasted or cruelly wrecked. Into my ward drifted intermittent echoes. At the epicenter, soporifics were distributed—three drams put us all down. Flogged into wakefulness, I yawned, dressed, broke into song on the wrong floor, slipped into sollerets.

Black hose hung like dead ducks. Placid approach to handwash. Labyrinth with drafts. Backwards-Midas, everything touched turned into a learning experience. I worked at the outlet store, sorting islands of contrivances. Cessation of sounds and voices, sky and sleep. Avoiding the stillness. Catching up on naming: cog for train and cog for arc and cog for dazzling and anticipate. The lost names not stopping me first.

Castle and moat or castle no moat or crag with castle or no castle just crag or crone laughter, thrown down the palace steps, for what was a palace but a castle without ramparts. Bones leading back to the dog, a dead end. Poems tapped out along the wires. Get out from under, let another species sit down. I entered many contests, submitted many forms, any combination of numbers and letters, a pause or a fall.

I learned light flour dusting, losing clean sleeves and pallid digits. Dry measure sped ahead of me, buttonholed by head wounds, rampant distractions, wrinkles assailed by every sort of plasty, a loose rendition of *What's My Line?* with Marie-Louise von Franz relearning the alphabet.

I kept a lock of my hair and a frying pan so I wouldn't confuse myself with my gramophone dream. The ferocious day came to an end. Mr. Sandman turned up at the Ritz. I was already in my starfish pajamas.

Under the bed, octopi, aperture or household tomb.

HELPING THE NEW GIRL

I HELPED THE new girl. I gave her clothes and some money. She looked human but never slept. She was kneeling near the wall, next to the water cooler. There were a thousand like her, all just as beautiful, all singing the same song. Only slightly different. The dress was a size too large for her. I couldn't let her go without a coat. She didn't have much interest in it. They took her down the hall and gave her a number. She sat in a chair. There were no lamps so she made the best of the dark. Don't go near the monitors, I said.

FROM A NOTEBOOK

1. I also might have died from a dog-bite wound. I could barely sleep anymore. Gloom made me do things I was sorry for. Numbers appeared again and again in clusters. Or when the phone rang and Fermi remarked, "By the way, is there any possibility of spin-orbit-coupling?"[1] I threw my cape to the ground, counted the crystals, the acute arrangement of atomic patterns, tossed away my bouquet of endangered languages and dialects.

2. The wound failed to heal and soon grew worse. It was the way the numbers announced themselves—as embolisms, not quantities. You'd think the soul would know it was dealing with numbers. The hearth had a fire and the walls of the boarding house brimmed with black and white flowers. My composure was lost. The prospect of symmetry was suspended then annulled. Here was the number six, or sleep, one plus two plus three, and one times two times three, a glow unfolding the darkness.

3. Cards held close to the chest—under the chest. I held the deuces, four aces, all zero cards. Dull lumps of estrangement and defeat. Liberties paid for with caution, my room let by the hour.

4. The pale yellow feathers on his tie.

5. *Contrary to custom I drank black coffee and could not sleep. Ideas rose in crowds. I felt them collide until pairs interlocked, so to speak, making a stable combination. It seems in such cases that one is present at his own unconscious work, made partially perceptible to the over-excited consciousness, yet without having changed its nature.*[2]

6. Mostly I remained myself but that became less the case. I was there, I'm sure. There was a place for me—same old stranger passing through, moving along the board with schemes and reasons.

7. In the end it'll be my hysteria or my highhandedness that'll get me up and running.

8. I had no doubt it was my mother who was trying to poison me. She assured me it was the only way out. There in my room, pitch black, no bigger than a closet. In one of my old china cups. In the wink of an eye I'd be dead. Then I opened the door, and there was the lunch counter, where a French physicist was trying to order meat in less-than-rudimentary English. I had a sudden lapse of faith about the poison. Wasn't there some other way? There wasn't, but I couldn't find the cup—I'd lost track of it.

9. What I needed was a neutral language to describe numbers. Perhaps you thought I was talking about sno-cones? I remember the reflection of the rowboat on the lake, *le petit canot*—all of

us doubled. Two, the first irrational number. Dance of identical particles. But it was my turn to be form and yours to be chaos. The day was full of trees and roots. What did I know of natural order? It was hardly discernible, let alone calculable, like the root of two.

10. The 'perfect number' was unknowable, though it molted to a point where it could be known—as a pair, an ensemble or a whole. Let the dead console slow learners. A step over the threshold and symmetry cannot be produced. A scuffle results— diagonals inside squares, rotations in six dimensions that appear as one.

11. Imitation was redoubled. The All-or-Nothing enters and, as soon as it does, splits into four, all of them telling us where they're going, and where they've just been.

12. Compass to myself, a deserter, wandering around the drum circle, counting the Indians, felling them like dominos. I was a medium not a face. When I let go, the wind lifted me up like a kite. This was not fruitless.

13. Libido, I observed, though not quantitative, became a rhythm, subliminal at first, then impalpable.

14. *We shall call the first part this and the second part that and the transition from one to the other we shall call neither this nor that.*[3]

15. Ideas which don't belong to any language like the rock scratchings in La Grotte des Fées or the arrangement of caves within a cave. Not artifacts but vibrations—a beat to be distinguished from its double.

16. The poison was a pharmakon and a whirlwind and a dial. The clock's four dimensions were visible as three.

17. Sound asleep like stones in the river.

18. We hoped to get results through geomantic spheres. But evidence could not be mediated by the senses.

19. We dreamt the model in reverse. There were no fractions, only zero and one, no repetitions, just it—dice coinciding with shooter.

20. Funnel-necked fruit jars, heroic giggles. The physical plane was of no concern to us now. Remember . . . a sequence or the primal arrangement of lines. As a calculation it was accurate. Circumference of a ballroom gown floating. Received ideas on the reception line by the door.

21. A last glimmer of sun melts childhood to sun. That's stretching it a bit. Periodicity is nothing but a rhythm.

22. Why should a melody strive? Here is the open universe. Here is the perfect cube. We've only to find another language. Any hole open.

23. Smoke. Embers sleeping feverishly, startled by the progress of the fire. The problem at hand: *vitesse-mouvement* ≈ *fréquence-mouvement.* "Coucou! Me voici!"

24. The concerted effort the dead will make to remember the living. Performance of post-mortem miracles, silent laments, synthesis with sevens tainted by constraint.

25. A menacing floor plan—shadows advancing. Flux, inadvertent light. I know how we got here. No one will sit by me, gazing out the window.

26. Applying gadgets to different parts of us, shocks which didn't feel like much.

27. A sweetheart hidden in the wash, or in the past.

28. Having been evaporated, or reabsorbed. No staying power— need something extra. Pay no attention to tiny Saint Sulpice. "Pineau des Charantes pour Madame, la Réserve Personnelle pour Monsieur." Are these spirits? Rearranging us?

29. A retrograde connection to linear sequence produced a casual unspooling of later and sooner.

30. It was only the Occident that regarded evens and odds as opposites.

31. The clock was the spot where we found ourselves stuck in the sum total of unknown possible conditions.

32. What was needed of course was *un mode d'emploi*, or an Idiot's Act of Chance, a primer to explain why time is only significant in becoming (*i.e.*, natural numbers).

33. A hairline crack in the lip of the cup supports the principle of the open system. We set forth an experiment in which the fluid would be emptied. The alchemists then suggested we leave space and time behind and enter the wormhole of *unio mentalis*, but the contact point, where psyche and matter were to meet, could not be agreed upon.

1. *Newsweek*, November 18, 1963.
2. Jacques Hadimard, *The Psychology of Invention in the Mathematical Field.*
3. D. Kharms, *On Time, Space and Existence.*

DORA'S SOLILOQUY

HOPE AWAKENS AND rearranges the room while we're sleeping. An instant later the lamps are relit and all is put the way it was. I leave it in your hands while I look for myself there. You trace the trappings, the debris leading back to me. Guilt is automatic. I myself am blind to it. Let's go back to the lake. I'm willing. To be born, to die, it's not the same thing. A slap in the dark, where am I? Only the bold strokes are here, edges of things. I won't pretend to think. Sound reasoning. You were advising me to listen *bitte.* The way a doll can listen. Tell me again, leave nothing out. Note for the record I've requested the statement be repeated. Or was it a question? Perhaps tomorrow I'll tell you the rest unconditionally. Tomorrow will be different. Perhaps not. I've spoken of the lake; what I say will be a secret, when I dream it, if that's possible. It's become a case, if not a story. It's a good thing we're dead. You were speaking for me? If I tell it myself, who will believe me? Prayers? That's psychology for you. It's the end. It's been restful. I'll tell you more when you write to me, my real name for instance.

ASYLUM

I SHOULD HAVE counted sheep but I didn't. The woman in the velvet cloak was eating honey-roasted peanuts from an animal bag, and the old man played the concertina in the station. I read a little while I waited. I couldn't concentrate, read the same sentence over again, tried not to think about it; time stopped, though I was sure night would pass; I was stuck in the book, couldn't raise my head to see the sun rising over the desert, clamor of dawn, slaughter, shadow. I stared at the ticket agent with nothing in mind. No distractions was my excuse to dawdle. Silence droned on like speech. No rubber shoes coming down the hall. My daydream ebbed . . . time (what are circadias?), where was it going? I was in a hurry, like a child with a particular toy picked out.

In the all-night diner, the little song of the branch tapped the glass. The waiter's sidelong glance at the man murmuring grace; at night it was the gaze that fell longest, not the embarrassed laugh, or terse rejoinder, boredom barely suppressed after midnight. Half-moon blurred, stepping out of traced lines, carried along uncomplaining. A travelling sort of pain, pensive or inscrutable, the blanket no use. When it came to thinking, I practiced at being natural. I needed a new coat. I looked like an artist. Was I some kind of dog? A half-hour in the café. No one should have to control it that long. The commonplace gesture, normal expression, nothing hotheaded, a slice of pie, but the right kind of pie—pretty. I miss my dream train, the one Mark Twain took through the Ganges. It was slow, no one's set their watch by it since well before Victoria died.

Typically, I was detained, just as I was distracted by the beautiful illusion of departure, like being pitched into the abyss, stressful though not intolerable. After all, the soul was purely epistemological, a wave from a dream car window.

If words are left out, there's silence, brief but unbearable. Any sound unsaid but listened for—numbers, waves, white noise. Not that I dwelled on the futility of speaking. In general I was capable of a whole range of feelings, dreading them. Sometimes I slept or else stayed awake reading true crime stories. Like any other woman, I had skirmishes with the commonplace. Lights off lights on and so on, planes droned in space, solitary constellation, bracketed but unchecked. Slogans, insurgency, rumor. For obscurity, substitute constraint. I read through the day or walked in the neighborhood or slept until night.

Time passed, I wasn't bored. Light passed, the dog barked or the telephone. It is raining and one part of the population tries to annihilate another. Was there a dog in my future? My sense of proportion had been slipping away like any other staple. The pharmacy wasn't stocking my soap anymore; I went wild with anxiety. That I could no longer carry on a conversation meant next to nothing. Except for the soap, I managed to keep all the pieces in place—ridiculous, I was playing right into the hands of apathy.

HUMORESQUE

MOTHER WAS THE first man I ever met. Behind the curtain of ciga-
rette smoke and Joy. His smell was everywhere at once. Not yet out
of the crib, I knew how to roll over and play dead. I learned every-
thing in reverse, first running, then baby steps, later crawling. That's
how I spent most of my time: feigning. I would stay away for weeks
at a time without being missed. But Mother stayed away even longer.
I didn't know what to do with all that time. I cultivated the art of
invisibility, putting myself in dangerous situations. I wasn't lost, I
was *unseeable*. Even my footsteps vanished after me. Next the people
disappeared, then the city.

I only needed to make myself unseen by myself, an impression.
Now and again there was a fleeting hint I'd been here before, what-
ever *here* was. As soon as I grew up I discovered important facts
about myself, *e.g.*, I may never have existed at all.

Sometimes the scream lasted a day, breaking the eggcup with
Napoleon's picture on it. The scream followed me to school and
learned the letters, while I sat dumbly in the back row.

Mother played Helen Morgan records while we went about our
business. By 'we' I mean me, or my brother who they said was a
prophet.

Mother dropped the soufflé and laughed. His laugh usually took care of everything. But not this time.

In the cellar is a pile of shoes. I imagine they are watching me. I pick a pair from the pile, scrape off the crud, and give them a shine. The next day, another pair, and so on, for months. One day, all the shiny shoes are gone.

There is also a lathe and a jeweler's saw and an old tobacco can filled with nails that have no secrets to tell me. And the hems of Mother's gowns. Later I sit with the old shellac under the stairs. I observe spiders with a flashlight. Little stars raking across fiber. They didn't take much interest in my light. Spiders bring luck, someone said. I didn't believe it.

PART I

THE DARK BACK room, like an invisible lining, no way of slipping out, no more than a synapse. Unnameable? Maybe. No rose by any name I know. Trace broken. Though no need to exclude a thing. No pleasure in knowing, only knowledge and knowledge of knowing. Like a woman. Not a real woman. What remains—leftovers. An eye gouged out but still part of me, the words turning circles. I mean the real woman. What the name's based on. Not sleight of hand, nothing for the beholder.

Wondering where the footpath went got me nowhere exactly. That didn't stop me from following it though there were no words for where it took me—I made them up. The first words threw over language. There were things to be named. I needed to think. What would answer me? The path was so overgrown I couldn't see my feet though I could imagine them. I called them *linkings*.

As far as I could tell, I wasn't trespassing. I suppose they wanted me to. It wasn't sacred ground or even virgin turf. But I doubted if I could find my way back.

No good to look for landmarks—the ocean pounded away as always, the weekend gone, passion, sticky stuff, aimless flashes— things that had always been there; I mistook them for myself. My mirror was one of those fish-eye family photos, like the hailing class of '22, only with everything under the sun in it. There were sounds, too. I heard them. They were pleasurable, affiliated with letters.

I tried for tree instead of *tendresse* (the word for it) leaving it for others to sort out. I found the word for happiness but it only meant cuticle (or largesse); tremble also meant puny. I was in the middle of a hieroglyph (or *phobia*)—condensing nameables and unnameables. *Tendresse* was an obstacle in a no-word zone. I followed the crumbs: egg, chicken, want, fear . . . another conundrum I called the *centobois* to keep from being frightened to death.

Next no trees, only lines, wires, on and on—attached to nothing in sight. Was I a tree? Giving up the gelcaps, the motion of phobia; in a blue pool, the reflection of a dryad. Define reflection. I needed my pixie tube to stay afloat—blew it up myself in the bath. Define breath. The notion of floating. Define water. X-rays, in a drawer. Always there. "Anti-definite." Crumbs in my hair, etc. Not what *they* like—pas propre, unclean, interdit, verboten.

Who needs a body?

PART II

WINGS WERE ON her list *("j'aime bien ton aile"),* so were earrings, her
darling shell dotted with jewels. In the temple: Great Lash Mascara,
drastic breasts—some sanctuary. Drifting down to the cellar to see
if it was locked, she got knocked off the toilet by the blast—
anthrax (or the Carpenters) passing over the plains at daybreak. A
tulle shawl in the scaly blaze. Lava, smoke. If only she could die,
like in the old days. A job prospect turns up at the cigarette conces-
sion at the foot of a volcano. Here is a complimentary fossil, a
token of our misgivings.

Awakened by a ghost in short pants—*what's with the toreador
get-up?* And the shadow of a boomerang on the sea. Or the chorus
of ducks who squawk moi non plus. Or the unusual prenuptial
impregnation of Derek Jeter by aliens. Whose fault? (In the paint-
ing contest, he was the only one to use glitter.) I don't *like* you, she
said, even though she knew he had come back from the dead.

Dirk: Still scribbling?

Lil: Scribbling—Christ!

Dirk: Gin?

Lil: Mm-hm.

Dirk: With . . . ?

Lil: With gin. Gin with gin.

Dirk: Tiny fizz?

Lil: Stiff! Fill it with gin!

Dirk: Right.

Lil: Twit!

Dirk (*mixing drink*): Plink plink plink. Dirk's kirsch . . . Lili's gin.

Lil: Bring it!

Dirk: . . . fixing this twist. I'm finishing—

Lil: Dirk's spilling it!

Liz: Still fighting?

Lil: I think fighting is thrilling.

Liz: Isn't it insipid, criticizing him?

Dirk: I'm winning!

Liz: Chilling tidbit.

Dirk (*sipping kirsch*): I'm tight.

Lil: Ripping.

Dirk: Drink, Liz?

Liz: Milk.

Dirk: Milk? Bit prim.

Lil: Dirk, Liz is six.

Dirk: Milk it is *(mixing it)*. Spritz? I'm kidding!

Lil: I'm finding this tiring.

Dirk: Did I blink?

Lil *(swigging gin)*: Wimp.

Dirk: Witch.

Lil: Prick.

Liz: This is sick.

Lil: I'm driving him wild.

Liz: Nipping his id?

Dirk: I'm winging it.

Lil: I might kill him first.

Dirk: Thinking big!

Lil: I'm thinking bright pink lipstick, g-string . . . I'm thinking
      I'll ditch him.

Dirk: Bright spirit? I insist.

Lil: I'm blind.

Liz: If living is this simplistic I think I'll skip it.

Lil: Nihilism is . . .

Dirk: . . . kitsch.

Liz *(whistling)*: It's midnight. I'm splitting—with Liszt.

Liszt: IRF! IRF!

I KNOW WHERE I'M GOING

NO NEED TO READ the paper that said Please Read This Paper. . . .
She hadn't read it once. Surely there must be some Law that Prevents the Worst from Happening, she thought. There was her practical fear with a rope and stone attached.

Her to-do list: smelling rain, then nothing.

She was making her way through the streets. Walking as she slept. She knew these blocks by heart. A dachshund pup snarled at her and threw up. She ducked into the overpriced bodega and bought a package of little chocolate donuts. On the radio, the topic was *terroir*. "Who's to say that an element of soil exhaustion does not contribute to finesse?" On the street, a little girl pointed at her. Her mother yanked her off the curb. That might have been the start of her melancholy.

She walked up First Avenue to Sutton Place to the little park along the East River. Couples were out in evening dress, black-gloved and minked. One of the minks winked at her as she stood in the shadows. Without seeming to be immodest, she had to admit she was not unattractive, short of being skinless. Maybe they'd toss her a bit of goose liver left over from lunch.

She was not an opium-eater nor devoid of sense. It was cold and she had a home and she went there, stopping at the store for a bialy. She popped the bialy into the toaster oven, looking over the book she was to proof; which had been dropped off by messenger. The book was full of pictures of women, all races and ages, some astonishingly beautiful. She felt weak yet kept turning the pages,

39

forgetting the bialy until she noticed tufts of black smoke wafting from the kitchen. Fire was the last thing she needed. She quickly took the glass of cognac she was drinking and threw it over the bialy, which sent flames shooting in every direction. There was nothing to do but run. She pounded on her neighbor's door. Old Mrs. Lamb, who could barely get up and down the stairs, had the fire out in a wink. She warned her to be more careful, that she was just an old woman and couldn't be running around putting out fires.

While the smoke was clearing, she went out into the night. They'd told her to stay out of the cold but she wrapped a scarf around her head and stumbled out. Now what? People milled about, avoiding each other, striving all the same.

She bumped her way along the street, past the funeral home and the thrift shop.

"Jane?" A woman's voice called from an open door. She peered into a brightly lit room. Gray chairs were stacked along the wall. Some had been unfolded in a rough semicircle. People were sitting in them. She entered, looking for the voice, and took a seat in the back. She could barely make out the profile of the speaker, his features obscured by heads nodding all along the row. Leaning closer, she could see his pasty hands working each word as he spoke it. He told them how glad he was to have his problem; she couldn't figure out why this should be so.

She'd been sitting in the room for twelve minutes. No questions asked, spent, but the needle at least hovering over the old grooves. You think you're downtrodden? Passing the time stitching socks? By anomie, I mean something so simple it has nothing at all to do with me. I'm fairly eclectic, nothing preventing it. English custom with its many serving pieces. In my case, euthanasia was mentioned. All glue but not a brick in sight.

"Where was I?" the speaker said, "I don't know. I'm moving, I'm on a bus—and I'll be damned if I know where I'm going." She was once on a bus, but she was only going to Cherry Hill to buy a mochi maker. She always knew where she was going. Once she went out to get the *Enquirer* and found herself downtown on Canal picking over old poultry shears. She always retraced her steps. She didn't like lapses. As far as she could tell, she'd never had a blackout in her life.

"I'm here today and today I'm here."

They applauded. "Thank you, Dale."

A woman raised her hand and began describing a visit to her in-laws during which she'd turned her will over to a higher power, without much success. The group nodded and folded their arms over their chests. A young woman to her left thumbed through a pamphlet for a passage, which she read aloud. More applause. What could *she* tell the group? There was the time her spleen had fallen off on the train. She hadn't noticed how inflamed it'd become. Was that her fault? She might've paid more attention but there were so many things to pay attention to.

"I know that if I weren't here today I'd be . . . in dialysis." Dale again.

My name is Jane and I despise you. Wisely, she refrained. She needed to find a way of slipping out. She shifted uneasily in her seat, aware of the stickiness beneath her. The group rose to their feet,

". . . accept what I can't . . . wisdom to know the difference." She placed the handout on the metal chair and caught the eye of a lion puppet propped on the edge of an easel.

"You know you'll never get anywhere with an attitude like that," he said. Yes, she knew that. "Nep nep nep nep nep," he repeated for emphasis.

She'd always duck out before the credits rolled. But tonight she missed her chance, they were already rolling, blocking the door. She thought of saying I don't *have* a problem. Or state soberly that she wasn't ready to talk about it. She was almost ready. "Ordeal," the lion cued her. I'd like to stay and chat but I have to go home and—*Slop-pail daughter*. Who said that? She began to feel damp all over. She was accustomed to not going out. I'm no intruder, she said. Oh no, you're certainly not. Had she said that? Sickening. Hello I must be going. And don't come back. Not for all the dermis in the world, she decided.

On the sewer grate, a black rat bared his teeth at her. Oh, it's only a rat, she told herself.

"It's only a rat," the rat mimicked. She turned onto the bright avenue, watching her breath cloud up. She became dimly aware of gasping behind her. A gloveless hand was on her sleeve. He looked at her without a trace of queasiness. She tried to avoid him but it was impossible. She found the space before her eyes, an immaculate blankness.

"Didn't I just see you at the group? Do you live near here?"

She was looking for the subway stairs. She wasn't used to conversation.

"I live over there," he said.

He meant the high-rise where a gold-braided doorman was blowing on his knuckles.

"Right there," he said, pointing to the sky. "The light is out but . . . you see that window there?"

She lived on one of the filthy side streets a few blocks up.

"Would you like to have a cup of coffee? Not at my place of course. My name is Dick." He held open the door to the coffee shop. "And I've been an abuser all my life—a *recovering* abuser for about . . . seven months—I should say 'a day', right? You're addicted to one thing, you're addicted to everything, yes? What was your name again?" he asked. They slid into an empty booth.

"Jane."

"Huh. Dick and Jane. Jane and Dick. Not bad." She excused herself and went to the bathroom.

Emptiness was a real sensation. First she rummaged through her pockets—she thought she felt a lymph node sticking to one of her mittens—then through her bag, and unearthed an ancient Zebra Cake, squashed, but still good. She wolfed it down, swabbed the creme from her jaw and dodged the mirror. When she returned, two steaming cups were on the table.

"Would you like a slice of pie?"

She paused before stating, "I don't like the unknown." It was the only thing she could think of saying. She dug her hand into her pocket, feeling the slippery clot.

"Neither do I," he replied. "Hate it. I plan never to die—never."

In truth, she didn't mind the unknown; it was him she didn't like. Once she realized that, she was fine.

"You have crumbs on your coat," he said, lightly brushing her lapels with the tips of his fingers. She flinched.

"What I like are *Tinea pellionella*."

"*Tinea pellionella*," he repeated.

"Moths," she pronounced.

"Oh yes," he quickly agreed, "Especially when they become butterflies."

"I was really thinking about their larvae eating woolen goods, and of course their nocturnal habits." He shook his head intently. "I don't understand why people hate them so," she continued. "When you turn on the light, and you can *hear* them batting their wings and flying right into the bulb—you really have to admire that."

Her speech was cut short by the babble of her small intestine taking the cake.

"Excuse me," she said.

"Certainly."

There was silence. Dick slid his hand across the table to take hold of Jane's. She snatched it away.

"I should be going." she said.

"Yes," Dick sighed. "I suppose we might as well be on our way."

He paid the bill. Jane walked quickly past the mirror that faced the counter. She headed toward home. Dick followed.

"May I see you again? Wednesday, say, after the meeting?"

She didn't answer.

"Then how about the weekend? Friday evening. In the park—not a bar. Four, four-thirty, five o'clock?"

"Oh, all right. Four."

"I can walk you home—right to your door."

"No, thank you," she said and turned the corner.

***

Did she have a mother? She couldn't see her face. It wouldn't materialize. If she had a mother she must have had a face, or a voice. She forgot what she was thinking. It was night, winter. Was she dreaming? She heard knocking on the door.

"Would you go down and get me a Pabst Blue Ribbon?"

"I'm not here."

"When will you be back?"

Jane didn't answer.

Mrs. Lamb had no understanding of doors. On the other hand, she brought her creme cakes and sometimes did her wash. The other day she brought her an issue of *Vogue.* Mostly, Jane tried to avoid her. She didn't need anyone looking after her. She was content. In the summer it was easy; she hardly went out. She would have liked to walk along the river. She wanted to go to a foreign country and drive a car. She wanted to go to a lake and put her face in the water.

Now she lay in bed listening to an LP: Tommy Dorsey. Dave Tough on drums. With the lightest of touches, Tough buoyed the whole band. She couldn't figure out how he did it.

She had to read the newspaper with gloves because of the ink. One day she would go away without a word. A man on the telephone asked her what brand of moisturizer she used. That'll be the day. She knew she had a sister who died before she was born. She had read about a theory stating that under the right conditions an entirely new life form could spring up.

She was listless but not tired. She turned on the television and fell asleep. There was a news report about a cult. She fell in with it. Aphorisms she couldn't understand appeared out of nowhere. The face of the leader was everywhere. He resembled Gene Krupa. The members held masks on sticks which they lifted to their faces. She realized she needed to put her shoes on the right feet.

She woke up to knocking.

"Are you home yet? I have some Pabst. The Arab boy brought it."

"I'm still not here."

"When will you be back?"

"I won't."

"Shall I come back later then?"

"Certainly not. This day is over. I'm going to bed."

***

Dick stared vacantly at the bare branches of the trees. Jane blinked to keep her eyes from watering and getting stuck.

"I didn't see you at the group on Friday. Are you going next week?"

"I don't think so."

'Why not?"

"I'm not really addicted to anything."

"Oh no, you've got to come."

Jane said nothing.

"Look, everybody's addicted to something. Have you heard of those people who love too much? You can even be addicted to *love*. Women love women too much, men love men too much. But I'm getting off on a tangent. There must be *something* you can't give up. You should really come."

"I'm not addicted to anything."

"I didn't used to think I was, either. One day this, the next day that. I was convinced I didn't need anything. See what I mean?"

She was watching a pigeon with a damaged leg hobbling across the stones.

"Wet Naps were the deal-breaker for me. One day I was in a foreign land. Not that I was addicted to travel. Though come to think of it, I took three vacations that year—perhaps you're right. Anyway, there I was with a beautiful young woman I'd paid lavishly to accompany me about, in one of their top-notch restaurants. They'd never even *heard* of Wet Naps. The maître d' was called. A hot washcloth was brought and so forth. I mean what could I do? I put my head down on the table and started to sob. I cried and cried. And do you know that the beautiful young woman who was my guest got up and walked right out. No 'bon soir'. No 'thank you so much for the escargots', no 'merci beaucoup for the Montrachet', not as much as an 'excusez-moi'. Can you beat that? But what did I care? A hole was ripping right through the middle of my life. Then and there I realized that it was bigger than just me. Get it? I guess you do. I think you see deep down that I'm right, right? But I'm running on again. Why don't *you* talk for a while? Not that I want to put you on the spot. What would you like to talk about?"

Jane stared down at a twig caught between cobblestones.

"Plankton."

"Plankton?"

"Yes. What's your favorite?"

"My favorite? I don't know . . ."

"Mine are *Physalia*, *Physalia physalis*, which really aren't plankton at all. Bluebottles. Portuguese man-of-war. In fact it isn't even an animal, but *four*. Four separate and discrete animals."

Dick's face was a blank.

"Each inseparable and totally dependent on each other. One part directs movement, another part catches food, the third part paralyzes the prey and the last part digests it and spreads it to all the other parts."

"But what about reproduction? There must be a 'part' for that?"

"No. Each one has male and female parts. The fertilized egg turns into larvae that bud asexually and produce a huge *Physalia* colony."

"Hermaphrodites?"

"Yes. But the tentacles are best of all. They're attached to this thin blue bladder that drifts around, and when the little fishes are swimming along they get all tangled up in these tentacle threads hundreds of feet long. Then the threads contract and drag them into the digestive polyps and they all turn into one big mouth."

48

Jane made a motion with her forearms and fingers to imitate the action of the tentacles, but caught herself and immediately thrust her hands into her pockets.

"It sounds ghastly," he said.

"All of the tentacle threads are really tiny tubes with triggers loaded up with barbs. And each one of those barbs contains a tiny stinging capsule that's absolutely toxic."

"I can't say as I'd like to run into one of those bottles."

"You'd better not. Even a dead or disabled man-of-war can cause great harm. Shock is one of the first symptoms—then intense pain, then a dull ache that extends to the joints."

"Sounds like a hangover."

"I've never had a hangover."

"Oh dear."

"I must get home," she thought, rising automatically and setting off.

"Where are you going?"

"I—"

"I was going to take you out to eat. At a very fine restaurant— big steaks, Bordeaux, that sort of thing. You're probably a vegetarian. I thought of that."

"I'm not."

"Fine, then let's get going. I've worked up an appetite listening to you talk. Not for fish, mind you. Ready to go? It's right around here, but we can take a cab, if we can find one. Oh, there, hurry, run."

"No."

"Come on."

"I'm not dressed."

"Yes you are."

"For dinner I meant."

"Oh that. Don't worry. Well, now that you mention it, perhaps we can stop along the way and you could pick something up. My treat, of course."

She had no idea why she was allowing herself to go along with him. Something in her had temporarily collapsed. He took her sleeve and led her out of the park and onto a street of stores.

They approached a high-end boutique whose window had no mannequins or display, only two or three garments swept across a short proscenium. The interior was all white, with very high ceilings. They waited for a young woman, all in white, to buzz them in.

"That's nice," said Dick pointing at a black crêpe-de-chine, off-the-shoulder number. "Or how about that?" snatching a lycra catsuit from the rack.

"Well, I would have to try it on."

"You can't try it on," the salesgirl said to Jane.

"Why not?" asked Dick.

"Store policy—no trying on."

"What are those white curtains over there? Aren't those dressing rooms?" said Dick. "I see . . . a silhouette—someone's taking clothes off and putting clothes on."

"Those are for *employees only*. That's an employee trying on."

"You have to buy the clothes to see if they fit?"

"That's correct. But, if they don't fit, you can return them."

"You can return them if they don't fit," he said to Jane.

"For store credit only. And provided, of course, they haven't been worn."

"But how can you tell if they fit without *wearing* them?" asked Dick.

"I'm just telling you our *store policy*. Once a garment is worn, you can't bring it back. So, now, do you want the garment or not? Because, if you do, I won't be able to hold it for you. Please decide now."

"Jane?"

"I don't want it."

"Yes, we'll take it. I'll write you a check."

"Visa and MasterCard."

"I've got a California driver's license plus a valid U.S. passport."

"We don't accept personal checks."

"Oh this is dreadful."

Jane was leaning against cubes of pullovers. Everything outside her was beginning to pulse. She thought, "Warm means wet and wet means cold." Then a familiar voice recited: "There was a little girl who had a little curl, right in the middle of—" and then it stopped short. "Make tracks baby." She was pushing against glass. "Buzzer!" the lion screamed and she was out the door.

She had never run before but she was running. Dick ran faster and caught up with her. She was out of breath. "I can't run."

"Jane, please don't spoil—"

". . . and I don't wear clothes. And I can't eat out."

"Jane, please——"

"I don't like you. I'm going home."

"Please don't go."

"Goodbye."

She turned the corner quickly and a bit of gristle flew off the nape of her neck. She glanced back to see if he were following; he was nowhere in sight.

***

Jane sat in the armchair watching Lamb gutting mullets.

"What about this man?"

"What man? Oh, you mean . . . he's not a man—I mean . . ."

"Is he in love with you?"

"I suppose so."

"*Suppose so!* You sound just like a prostitute the way you talk. This one and that one and that one and this one."

"Please don't say that."

"I was young once, but I was never a tramp."

Jane rose to her feet. "Excuse me, I'm going."

"I thought we were going to play cards."

"I'm sorry, I just remembered something I have to do."

"What about the tea? I made it for nothing?"

"Oh, all right, let's play."

"Don't you say 'I'm sorry?'"

Jane stared.

"If he knew you like I know you he wouldn't want to go out with you."

"I don't want to go out with *him.*"

"Of course you don't. He's probably an axe-killer with a wife and six children. I'm so old and tired."

"You must be close to eighty."

"I am not. Would you like to see my marriage certificate? I haven't got one!" She rummaged in her purse and extracted a ragged scrap of paper.

"Here's my New York State driver's license!"

Jane held it under the lamp on the end table. "It says you're eighty-four. You don't look your age."

"Yes, they say the weather is going to change. Play something for me on the cello."

"I can't play the cello."

"Yes you can. I heard you."

The doorbell rang.

"Would you get that, dear? It's probably my rice pudding."

Jane got up and opened the door. A young man in a khaki outfit, holding a clipboard, stood in the hall. He winced when he saw Jane.

"Mrs. Lamb, you've got a package. Shall I sign for you? It's from your sister. She sent you a box of honeybells."

"Florrie?"

"Mm-hm."

"My God. Eighty years and she can't remember I hate oranges."

Jane examined the tangerine-headed figures decorating the box. One of them was shaking maracas.

"Play something for me on the flügelhorn."

"I can't play the flügelhorn. I could play the tom-tom, or the bongos, or the conga drum, or the snare. Or how about the marimba?"

"Go! No, don't leave me! I thought you were going to play nocturnes for me."

"You know I hate to play the piano."

"You play beautifully."

"I won't play. Besides, you don't even have a piano. I play the drums. Can't you remember that?"

"I'm an old woman . . ."

"You can remember the words to songs no one's sung for fifty years. You can remember exactly how many rounds of rummy you've won and by how many points. You remember which fish I've brought you the week before because it's always the *wrong* fish. And you remember all my many shortcomings which you recite to me without end. Every time we have tea, you recall the cup I accidentally broke six years ago. You even remember my birthday, and every year you tell me it's the wrong time for girls to be born."

"Well, dear, that's true. April is a very bad month for girls. The worst girl I ever knew was born in April. And you did break that beautiful china cup—you think I could forget a thing like that? And you do always bring me the wrong fish. I ask for cod, you bring me carp. I ask for salmon, you bring me snapper. How many games

I've won? That's easy, you *always* lose. As for your shortcomings, you know I only point them out to you because I'm trying to *help* you. But how do you expect me to remember every little whim of yours? Do you think I care whether you play the Jew's harp or the kazoo? Do you think I spend the whole day thinking about you?"

Jane crossed the room and walked out the door, stifling an impulse to slam it. A moment later she opened the door and announced, "I will not impose my ichthyological *whims* upon you any longer. You can get your own fish!" This time she did slam the door.

***

The letter lay on the floor between the door and the rug. She saw it but made no move to pick it up. She opened the window a crack and went back to her book. Finally, she tore open the envelope and unfolded the blue notepaper.

Dear Jane,

I never guessed I would have to write you a letter like this but we are in conflict with each other. Conflict is also a form of antagonism upon which partnerships are built. One against the other can only lead to one for the other. Just as every misstep is also a step.

I admire your independence and grisly logic. It is also dangerous. What can be the basis of our reconciliation? As such, I recognize my mission is not to make you sanguine but to show you I am resigned.

Earlier in life I thought I might have made my nest with some-one lovely. And yet at times I sense that it was you who I was destined for. I have long since recognized the impossibility of bliss and wish to stick with someone who knows the flavors of sin, whose head is bent in sorrow and tranquility. Love will not make us happy as life has not. I will not affirm that I love you, nor will I disavow it. Maybe I am on surer footing with renuncia-tion, with an emphasis on candor.

I am on the precipice, climbing back from a deep chasm. I do not mean to deny the obvious.

There remains the potential for metamorphosis. Though you are far from it now. Thought and action cannot be underesti-mated. (Also the group.)

If you would like we could move to New Jersey. There are groups there you know. We will choose in good time. There will be some things I won't like about you and vice versa. This is the road to progress.

We are offered a choice. Multiple choices. It's never one thing or another. Concealment is at the heart of the matter. Having your cake, not eating it. Later eating it secretly and not having it.

To close, this, on original sin: expulsion from paradise is final. We can never go back there.

Affectionately,

Dick

***

Once she imagined herself a normal woman, even a beautiful woman, who took off all her clothes before a stranger. One with a camera. It still shocked her to see men and women with their cloth-ing off; it always made her feel "undressed," though mostly she hardly thought about it, except when something fell off.

She remembered the doctor who had poked and jabbed her. "Perfectly normal. . . ." he said in a thick accent. Normal? The spasms in her solar plexus? Courtship (the idea) appalled her. Who could blame animals for mating selectively? Yet there was something plainly unnatural about human cohabitation. She saw them in the super-market, one pushing, the other gathering and grabbing, the two badly dividing or duplicating life's labors. Maybe if she were rightside out she'd adjust to drudgery.

Is sex the carrot that drives the cart? She supposed it was plea-surable, but why so important? Words work just as well. Could it be like reading a book? She liked to read travel books and could easily imagine herself in Padua, Beaune, Hokkaido or Bath. She never noticed how long she was "gone." She also forgot that she couldn't go out for more than an hour or so, especially in the winter, the summer, or in the rain or in the wind.

Could anything be as good as drumming? So what if she couldn't play with others? She drummed along with drummers on records—groups and bands. She had ears—after a fashion. She knew how music was put together and pulled apart; she felt herself riding in-side it. She could almost taste it and touch it. And *watch* it. Best of all, she never thought about it.

***

She heard a thumping. Who's that? Lamb again? No, her knocks were loud raps, sometimes progressing to kicks, which didn't let up until she answered. This was a light staccato triplet, followed by nothing. She waited. The same tentative taps again. No use pretending she wasn't home. She got up and opened the door. It was Dick. He stood stock-still, hugging a large parcel.

She thought of shutting the door quickly, but didn't.

"This is for you," he said, holding out the bundle.

"What are you doing here?"

"I followed you home, you see——that night. When you ran away. I waited in the street for your light to go on. I just buzzed your neighbor. I told her I had a package for you."

He picked up a record jacket. "I didn't know you liked music. I like it, too. Though not this sort of music."

"Please go."

"All right. I just wanted to give this to you."

"I don't want it."

"I went back to the store and bought it. I hope you like it. If you don't . . . well, you know. Perhaps we can go out . . . sometime, and you can wear it." He put the box down on the floor next to the door.

"No!"

He bolted through the hall and vanished down the stairs.

She closed the door and sat down on the bed. She studied the package, a glossy white box with a red ribbon. The longer she looked at it, the bigger it got.

"Get rid of it," a voice said.

"Yes, I know." There was no time to lose. She slipped on her coat, her mittens, her ski mask and was out the door.

Mrs. Lamb's door opened as she crossed the corridor. "That's the way you go, with the music on?"

"Yes," she answered. "I'll be right back."

It was dark out. She hadn't expected it. What if they're closed? she thought. She could just leave it on the street. No, she had to return it and give him the money—or store credit. "I'll leave it with his doorman. I know where *he* lives, too."

She entered the store without buzzing as two stylish women were leaving. "*Ce n'est pas vrai!*" one exclaimed to the other. The young woman in white was standing in the middle of the store with her arms folded. She had added a white velour turban, which Jane thought silly. She turned her back to Jane and began arranging jackets on a rack. As she approached her, the girl walked to the other side of the store and began fidgeting with CDs. Jane followed.

"Excuse me." There was no response. "Excuse me," she tried again, louder, placing the box on the counter between them. "I'd like to return this, please." She nudged the box toward her.

The girl glanced at the bag and began shifting sunglasses in a display case. "I cannot refund merchandise. I can give you store credit or let you exchange—"

"I'll take credit."

". . . provided, of course, the merchandise hasn't been worn."

"I haven't worn it. I haven't even taken it out of the box."

The girl examined the box. Jane noticed a small envelope tucked under the ribbon and snatched it.

"This hasn't been opened," she said accusingly.

"Yes, that's just what I said."

"How do you know this is *our* merchandise?"

"I was here the other day—with a man. . . ." Jane pulled the ribbon off the box and shook out the contents. The dress slid onto the floor. The salesgirl picked it up and placed it in the box.

"It didn't fit?"

"No. I didn't try it on. I just don't want it."

"Where is the receipt?"

"I don't have the receipt. It was a gift."

"Then I can't give you credit."

"The tags are still on it. I haven't touched it."

"No receipt, no credit. That's store policy. How do I know you haven't stolen this?"

Jane placed one hand on the display case to steady herself. "You think I've stolen this . . . dress from your store and now I'm taking it back for an exchange?"

"Why not?" the girl said, shaking her head disdainfully.

Jane torqued her body, flung back her right arm and, with all her strength, swung it around for an open-handed slap. There was a loud crack across the mouth and nose, causing a stream of bright blood to gush from the girl's face and splatter her white chemise.

Jane couldn't stop her legs. They carried her to the exit, where her burning hand found the buzzer. She ran swiftly out and down the street. From a distance, she heard loud sobbing. She didn't turn around.

She felt weak and strong.

***

The following day the light had changed. It was spring light, though the trees were still bare and it was cold. She made her way through the city. She wandered alone. She'd never been to Harcourt Brace. This was a rush job. It needed a quick turnaround. There were no messengers to be had.

She looked up at the sky. The first little flakes settled in her hair. A guy was going to ask her for directions then he saw her and said sorry. Please go away. She had forgotten the address, of course. Avenue of the Americas. A fountain out front with a statue of Philly Joe Jones. Or was that next door? She found it.

Inside, security waved her by. She was far too conspicuous to pose a threat. The elevator was cozy and warm and speedy. They handed her the envelope and quickly turned away. See you. It was a self-help book. She wasn't looking forward to reading it.

And now, a few words about copy editors: condescending, self-important, petty, mean, stupid, backbiting, sententious, officious, meddlesome, repugnant, unctuous, fatuous, malignant, pustulant, pestiferous, nitpicking, cynical, vitriolic, shallow, insensitive, malicious, odious, wicked.

The copy editor told her "no editing." She would never edit. She saw things to edit but she didn't do it.

She walked along looking up again. The second and third flakes drifted down. She couldn't feel them. She walked in the street against the traffic. The cars were silent and slow. Her mask was dusted in white. Like a Noh mask. She walked all the way home, reciting the state capitols: Frankfort, Bismarck, Salem, Pierre, Dover, Carson City, Concord. She loved all the chambers of commerce.

Did she have the envelope? Yes, tucked under her arm. Mrs. Lamb's light was on. Jane tiptoed up, turning the key and opening the door without making a sound. She didn't hear anyone moving about or the sound of the radio. Suddenly a voice a few inches away said, "Is that you?"

"No, it's not."

***

"I'm eighty-four, still going strong. Eighty-four. It's all in the past. Thank God. This tablecloth is a real beauty. It makes me feel less alone, this cloth. My Aunt Ruthie gave it to me. No—I took it, she was dead. Just look out that window, will you? Filth! I love to get up and go to the butcher's. I don't take meat; it's not ladylike. Oh I'll eat a goulash on occasion. The main thing is to get out. Shall I sing you a song?

> *"I'll be hard to handle*
> *What else can I be?*
> *Just ask my ma the problems*
> *She had controlling me."*

Mrs. Lamb picked out an old shellac record from a stack, blew off its dust and put it on the Victrola.

"Glinka! Wonderful! They don't make 'em like that anymore.

Rubbish! I used to go out with a boy. He looked just like Randolph Scott. He had his eye on me. Oh what's the use of talking about it."

She lifted the needle. "I saw your beau today, on the street. He was wearing a pink suit! Heh, heh! What a voice he has! Like an old chicken!"

She made a flapping motion with her arms. "Buck! Bucka-bucka-buck!"

"He's not my beau!"

"And the suit! I need a suppository. Hard to believe. Oh what remains. . . . A little cream soda?" She took a bottle from the refrigerator and poured two glasses.

"Of course the iceman came twice a week. Who could afford a fifty-cent block? You forgot the tray! You want a flood? Always with her nose in a book. And peach pits on the sofa. What was his name? Arthur? Izzy? My God! She used to make her own jam. Big pots . . . and the steam! It all had to be done so fast—boom! boom! The gooseberries are gone, too. What happened to them? I could've been happy with him in the Rocky Mountains. Florrie went instead. What happened to them? I got a card."

She handed Jane an old coaster. "Here."

"I don't want it."

"The radio is broken. . . . I had to go to the hospital, you know. The Ruptured and Crippled Hospital. Every week and even that wasn't enough. And all that was going on. He took me to dinner and a show and dancing. Don't flatter yourself, because my feelings for you have ceased."

"What?"

"This is you holding that pretty bone cup in your mitt. And when you spill it, well, all that, all that, my cloth's seen worse. You and your meat face. Go see your chicken-man. Poor creature. Take my stole, if you don't bloody it up. Go on, slink away. Our hearts were young and gay . . . a chicken in every pot! Why don't you sit down? Oh you are sitting down. I feel so tired. . . . Will you listen to that wind out there? I haven't had breakfast you know. You don't care. You have your mind fixed on that chicken beau of yours."

"Oh, please!"

"See how I know you? I haven't had a bite in hours. Lotsaluck!" She opened the refrigerator and inspected its contents.

"The doctor says don't eat herring, Maisie . . . so much misery. Just listen, would you? You don't have to speak. The whole thing's swimming in jelly."

"'Cause jam don't shake like that!" The lion let out a giggle.

"You stay out of this! Mind your own beeswax!"

"Bee-eezz!"

Mrs. Lamb leapt across the coffee table and throttled the lion. She wrestled him to the couch. They rolled onto the floor. The lion appeared to be enjoying himself. They got up and took a quick turn around the room. They danced and sang.

"A little dance, a little prance, a little seltzer in your pants!"

"I'm exhausted," Jane said. "I'm going to take a nap."

"I'm fine, you just run along," Mrs. Lamb replied.

"I'll just run along."

Jane went back to her apartment and fell asleep.

***

64

In the middle of the night the phone rang. She picked it up.

"Jane," the slurred voice said, "Jane . . . it's me, Dick."

She thought of hanging up.

"Jane, I was thinking of you. You. You and your bottles and your teeny pepinellas . . ."

"*Tinea pellionella*," she corrected him.

"*Tinena* . . . whatever."

"You're drunk," she stated.

"No-o-o. I'm in love—with an Armenian man-o-war . . ."

"Portuguese."

"Portuguese, Belgian, New Zealand. It's all the same my darling, you see that, don't you?"

"No."

"No? You don't? Yes you do. I know you do. I know you—"

"No. You don't."

"Did you know I was standing outside your house looking up at your window?"

"When?"

"All my life. . . ."

"You skipped your meeting then?"

"Nyehhh . . . I went to the meeting! You were there? I didn't see you! 'My name is Dick and today I'm abstinent'—well that was *that* half of the day. . . . 'My name is Dick and *this* half of the day I'm *not* obstinate . . . and I'm giving *all* my self-control . . . to higher power . . . here, *you* keep it for a while!'"

She listened to him laugh. She could almost smell the liquor. Then he stopped laughing and there was only breathing on the line. She hoped he wouldn't cry.

"Jane, I . . . I want a garden with worms and slugs and I want *you* there, too. To forgive my trespassing as I obey you, to take me to the train station and to pick me up. I'll tell you about my day dear and the years will go . . . pass quickly. You'll take up archery. The dog dies. The children—"

"Stop!"

"Don't worry dear, I'll do the cooking—I know how. After dinner we'll play cards and you can spank me if I lose—"

"Spank you?"

"Well, if you want . . . if I displease you, if you'd *like* to . . ."

"Dick, I have something very important to tell you." She spoke slowly and deliberately. "So, please, listen carefully."

"What is it, dear?"

"Never, ever contact me again—under any circumstances." She slammed down the receiver. She was so angry that her tear ducts began to dilate. But nothing came.

***

She sat down on the floor next to the bed, resting her head on it. She stayed there for a long time, even after she realized that one side of her face was stuck to the fuzzy blanket. Finally she got up, put on her coat and mask and went out. She walked. She walked down one street and then another. The streets were empty except for dealers skirting the park and people sleeping inside boxes or under scaffolding. She peered into first-floor windows and saw TVs flickering. She thought she might go to a movie, but the last shows had already begun. A hatless girl whose face and hands were red from the cold approached her.

"Give me a quarter so I can get something to eat," she said.

Jane fished in her pocket and handed her a Zebra Cake. She could see that the girl was disappointed. Jane realized that she was hungry herself.

"Would you care to have a bite to eat with me?"

"No thanks, mama. I got to meet somebody. Hey, I like your mask."

Jane turned onto Second Avenue. The Ukrainian National Home was open. She wandered into the empty restaurant.

"Sit wherever you want," the waitress said.

She left her coat at one of the tables and went to the back to find a bathroom. She needed a place to clean herself up, to pick the black lint from the mask off her face. She walked down a short corridor and pressed opened a door. It was dark. She fumbled for the light switch.

She stood at the edge of a large room with paneled walls. A chandelier and a big mirrored ball hung from the ceiling. Folding tables and chairs were pushed against the walls. The walls were covered with mirrors and oil paintings of Spanish dancers.

She went down a few steps, walked to the middle of the hall, and stood underneath the mirrored ball. She noticed some instruments set up on a small stage: an electric piano, a set of drums, several mikes and amps.

"Excellent," she said, moving toward the bandstand. She sat down behind the drums and picked up the sticks.

She began with a series of single bounce rolls and paradiddles at different tempos, then moved the patterns around the set, playing tiffs off the tom-toms and the floor tom. She threw in straight eighths on the bass and put the sock on the two and four. She followed this with some long press rolls and a second line snare rhythm, which she parlayed into a series of interconnected improvisations. She could hear a voice cueing her on rhythm patterns. Then it was just her, deep in the pocket. Maybe it had something to do with being inside out. She had to be extra-careful. She couldn't just let herself go. Her skin was buried deep inside her.

The sticks slipped from her hands and clattered across the floor. The waitress and the manager stood by the door.

Slowly she refocused on the room. She saw the red dots all around her. They speckled the drumheads, the pedals, the keyboard, and were scattered on the floor. A bit of frayed tissue was stuck to an amp.

She rose and wavered for a moment. Blood had dribbled on her shoes. The waitress and the manager stared at her. She rushed past them, grabbed her coat, and ran out into the cold.

***

What next? Lying in bed in the afternoon for as long as possible. Forget everything. It was comforting. Jackhammers banged outside her window, men shouted. Daylight scissored through the blinds. Fists balled up snugly. Restful. Her lids came unstuck, too weak to hold onto sleep. It slipped away from her like a dirigible. Where was it going? Now it was only a speck. She was awake. Things stuck to her: quilts, pillows, lint, spores. Eyes open, she propped herself up. The noise outside stopped at once. A plane passed over, then it was quiet again.

She reached out for her jacket and dug through the pockets, hoping to find a jawbreaker or some malted milk balls left over from the movies. She hadn't been to the movies for months. She found a small envelope with her name scrawled on it. "I am your friend and not your enemy and so much more," the note read. She ripped it up and threw it out.

A door slammed in the hall. Mrs. Lamb was groping her way down the stairs. The phone might ring but she'd never pick it up. Ever. She would not answer knocks or buzzes either. It was habit not need that led her outside. Each day she would resist the urge to go out. She was thirsty. She could go for a Yoo-hoo. She filled a glass with tap water and waited for resolve.

She thought. Was Dick thinking of her now? Pressing the sleeve of his shirt, envisioning their life together in New Jersey? That was all for the subject of Dick. He wouldn't pester her again. If I pass him in the street, I'll look the other way. I didn't see you at the group, he'll say. I won't reply. I won't let him touch my sleeve. He'll wring his hands, oh dear, oh my, oh no. With leaflets sticking out of his pants. Or a package. No. She wasn't going out so there was no possibility of running into him. He might come knocking again, but she would hold her breath. It was that simple.

69

Why was the pillow wet? She wasn't sad. Animal stories were what made her sad. She couldn't watch them; she'd dehydrate. Happy? As a clam? She was calm. The room was in order though it still smelled of smoke. There were the periodic attacks, somatic lapses.

It was cloudy but warm for March. She got out of her pajamas. She examined the Tiny Dancer plant she'd brought home a while back. It was dead. A pigeon landed on the windowsill, hobbled from one end to the other, then sat down. She cracked opened the window and a warm breeze blew in. I'm going outside, she suddenly decided. "Until we meet again," she said to the bird. "Adios," it replied.

She reached the platform as the train was pulling in. She was just able to press through the turnstile before the doors closed. She hadn't determined yet where she was going. Maybe she would go to Coney Island and walk along the shore. The last time she was there she ate cotton candy and got it all over her hands, face and coat. She'd gone to a palm reader, who took one look at her and screamed. This time she would avoid the amusement park. Rides were out of the question. She didn't like being jostled, or turned upside-down. She wanted to see the sea, and especially the horizon. Maybe if she could see where the sea touched the sky she would know what to do next.

The train was almost empty when she got on. At one end sat an old woman in a babushka. She went to the opposite end of the car, sat down and fell asleep. She woke up with a start. The train was standing still and the doors were open. The babushka had vanished. She wandered out into the pale light. The high-rises were gone and so were the tenements. There were only homes with shabby yards. A bicycle suddenly came flying at her. She thought, "I'm going to get knocked down now," as it swerved to dodge her. A sack full of rolled-up papers spilled onto the street. "Hey! Watch where you're going!" the boy shouted, gathering *Mirrors*. She leaned against a fire hydrant opposite a bait-and-tackle shop. "No Standing" the street sign said. "I'm not standing," she thought. "No getting comfy!" the sign replied.

She went into the bait shop. A man behind the counter was taking tiny objects out of boxes and putting them back again. She couldn't tell if he were counting; he was oblivious to her. She stepped up to the counter and took off her glove. He didn't look up. She cleared her throat loudly.

"You don't want nothin'."

"Yes I do."

"What?"

"Hooks," she said, fastening on the first object she saw.

"What size?"

"Medium," she said.

"Ain't got medium."

"What precise sizes do you have?"

"Got every size. What do you want?" He was a scrawny man with coke-bottle glasses, who looked over her shoulder when he talked.

"I don't believe he can see me at all," she thought. "Do you have any assorted hooks? A starter set, of sorts?"

"That'll cost you $9.95, plus tax, but it's got your weights, floats, fly-bait and wire. You want that?"

"Why not?"

"You plan to fish fresh or salt?"

"Salt."

"Then this won't do you a lick of good."

"I'll take it anyway."

"You got a reel? How 'bout a pole? You want them, too?"

"No thank you," she said.

"Don't like you," he mumbled handing Jane her change.

"Really? Why not?"

"You're the kind that keeps the minnows and throws back the bass."

"That isn't so," she said.

"Git now, I'm closed."

***

Jane walked down one street and up another. They were all the same. She knocked on the door of the house she liked best, the one most run-down. Someone was likely to be home. A tall woman in her forties opened the door. She was dressed in a herringbone skirt and a short-sleeved, coral sweater that clashed with her red hair, which was pulled up and pinned in a twist. "What do you want?" her expression said.

"I'm lost," Jane said.

"You're also inside out."

"I know that."

"Do come in."

There was only a narrow flight of stairs leading to a door; the downstairs part of the house had been walled off. She followed the woman up the stairs and through the door. "Who was that?" someone called from another room.

"Not *was* but *is*." She led Jane into a drafty room furnished with a card table, two unmatched wooden chairs, and a dilapidated sofa. A picture window looked out on the ugly street. A small woman dressed in chic but old-fashioned apparel rose from the sofa and held out her hand.

"May I present Mrs. Phayer. Mrs. Phayer this is . . ."

"My name is Jane."

There was an expectant pause but she said nothing more.

"My name is Miss Bang, as you may know."

"I don't follow . . . I mean, I *don't* know."

"Well, never mind, please sit down."

"We weren't expecting a visitor, but I'm awfully glad you appeared," said Mrs. Phayer. "It's been a rather dull day, with the post arriving late, as usual."

"Jane is lost."

"Ah," she sighed, "I'm so sorry. I was lost once. But then I made the acquaintance of prostitutes and actuaries, in a foreign land, and became estranged from my husband and former convictions and drank a good deal. That's when I began to be found again."

73

"This isn't a novel, dear. She's inside out."

"How unfortunate."

"May I take my coat and hat off?"

"Why, yes. And you mustn't be concerned about ruining the upholstery. This is all quite provisional, as you've probably noted."

"But the light in the morning in this room is enchanting."

"But you know one day we must leave this house."

"But why, Catherine? I do love it here."

"Mrs. Phayer, you know that it will be necessary."

Outside, the sky had darkened and the streets were one solid shadow.

Jane glanced at Mrs. Phayer, who was poring over a letter. It was handwritten, on notepaper that was dog-eared and yellowed.

"If you would like to make this your home—for the time being at least . . ."

"But I can't stay here."

"Do you have a pressing engagement?"

"Are you a prostitute?" asked Mrs. Phayer.

"No. Do you know where I am?"

"Certainly not."

"Well, goodbye."

The women began talking to each other as if she were no longer there. They were soon oblivious to her presence.

Jane left the house quietly. She heard the rumble of the subway and, in the distance, the rumble of thunder. She followed the sound of the train and reached the station just as the first heavy raindrops struck.

When she got home, she stopped and stood on the sidewalk for a moment. Then she sat down on the wet stoop. A thin girl with spectacles led her bicycle through the slush along the curb. She stopped when she saw Jane.

"What are you staring at?" Jane asked.

"Nothing."

"Yes, that's what I thought." She gazed at Jane intently.

"Would you like to play a game?" Jane finally asked.

"I'm too old for games. Is it fun?"

"How would we know that without playing it first? Wait here a moment."

Jane went up the steps and into the house. Presently she returned with sheets of plain paper and some colored pens.

"Now you draw me, and I'll draw you."

"Right," the girl said, removing her mittens and picking out red and purple pens. She scribbled furiously for several minutes. Meanwhile, Jane produced a fair rendering of the little girl.

"This is you," said the girl, showing off her work.

"Have you ever heard of psychology?"

"Of course. My parents are divorcing and I go to a psycholotrist two times a month."

"Just as I thought. Because in psycholotry there's a rule that says whatever you think another person looks like—fat, skinny, princess, dog—is how you yourself look. And judging by your drawing, I'd say you have a rather low opinion of yourself."

"This is not how *I* look, this is how *you* look."

"I think not."

"It *is!*"

"Not. Just ask that psycholotrist of yours."

The girl looked at Jane's drawing and then at her own. Her cheeks flushed with rage. She was holding back tears. All at once she tore up the picture, ran down the steps and sprang onto her bike. She'd ridden to the corner before Jane reached the door.

***

Jane lay on her bed and thought. This was the way things were. You went from day to day without letting your problems get in the way. She didn't mind hers that much. She had a job and she had her drums. She suffered when a sharp gust of wind hit her bare face. But then it was gone. Was everything like that? Here and gone? And of course there are always others with troubles worse than yours. She had no skin but at least she wasn't dead. In another time, she would have been a creature in a sideshow. People were caught up in their woes. They made a regular sport of it. In her case, she knew she couldn't change. It was all a matter of chance— mechanical laws of physics and biology, random but predictable.

She thought about her death. She couldn't feel it anywhere, even in her mind, it was so strange. She knew that one day she wouldn't put on her mask, or play her drums anymore. She imagined herself lying underground in a box. It was dark and cold. Then she thought that if she were reincarnated she might come back with some casing.

Someone was kicking the door.

"I made some biscuits. Open up."

Jane held her breath. Mrs. Lamb's biscuits tasted like clumps of dirt. Jane reached out and quietly turned off the light. Lying in the dark, she listened to Lamb go away. She remembered she had to go downtown the next day for her walker's license. She thought about riding in a warm taxi all the way down to the tip of the city, then she fell asleep.

***

Jane woke up early. She walked from the apartment to the station and took the train. It was full of high school students yelling at the tops of their lungs; her head began to pound. She got off near City Hall and walked to the state government building to have her walker's license renewed. People scurried all over the plaza. She felt something burning in her chest. A large woman in a man's suit bumped her and almost knocked her down. "Sorry," she mumbled, and she disappeared in the crowd. Jane walked up a ramp to the entrance.

The revolving door. Some people were circling in vain. Jane liked that. When she was little she went around and around. There were four quadrants. You pushed but you were being pushed. There was urgency. And when it was still it was odd. The rubber guard stopped flapping. But not for long. Her eyes cast down fastened to the floor. A burst of air then nothing, light, and then again, a wash carrying her along, no volition, feet tipped up, stuttering on their own. And the air slapped her at every go-round. Big bodies behind her, in front of her. Shoulders arms waists buttocks. The rubber whoosh pushed through. The music of dragging and sucking, striving against the undertow, never prevailing, losing her sea legs, vertigo, spilling. Pulling. Being born in reverse. Floor a blur of speckled burgundy. And the footsteps in red. Balance was out of the question. Others rushing out pushed. Stop me. It was on the tip of her tongue. Stop me if you've heard this one.

Don't push. There's plenty to go around. Stepping out of herself. She remembered the squished insect wriggling in the driveway. Wrong turn, the bottom long gone, ambulance slowing. The assemblage around her, vacant gaze of the driver, time readjusting itself. In a heap for a while. Subsistence. Languishing in rhythm. Dazed, making up for life. What? Were the paramedics waiting for the weather to change? Sun to come out from behind the clouds? Now I've seen everything. Hello My Name Is Jane, ascending colon snagged in the rubber. At intervals she recalled she was living. Though insensible, incrementally incapable of sorting source and issue, sauce and tissue. Entering the little boat. What difference difference? She could accommodate sameness. The nature of her state. Trachea trampled. She had access to the moment and the moment again, then no access.

A fractious instant of clarity, or convention. Her heart wasn't in this. But almost everything else was: hip ligaments, brachial plexus, sacral plexus, nerves, veins and arteries. Sitting upright, they wouldn't let her back down. Owing to mobile transfusion, monitoring, pulse, surfeit of regulators. On the whole a peaceable relapse. But it was all jumbled up. They watched from where she couldn't see them to

make sure nothing worse would happen. A vigil, though impersonal—that's the way they save you. Followed by plans for the
future: chances. General pandemonium of transport. Counting on
her fingers. What fingers? What was she counting? Starts and stops,
not coming to a complete stop, standing until the cars divided,
waters parted, then pressing on. The siren sang.

Fists balled with the thumbs outside for once. The worst was
over and done with or yet to come.

***

After hours. Engine turning over, light trickling in under the
door, little boat crawling. Numbness resumed. A low hum, time
filled in by the sea, adjusting to drumming, incessant humming,
light flaring up, dying down. She followed the fuzzy line separating
sea and sky, ragged but palpable, though she was too numb to touch
it. Getting used to the numbness. Taking in the grid—the coordinates were missing—and the rasp, "Man, this chick's done for,"
segued into space. Space spread out to shadows, then mystery. She
pushed off from the edges of herself and everything else, upstream
against others, to some calm tarn, sleep. At last, the vacation she
had planned, skiing in her old skin in Kitzbühel, a natural end. But
the hum of the little boat, rocking, knocked her about. Now to
rejoin herself already in progress. She opened her eyes—many loose
threads. She paused and stupor found her again.

As seen from afar . . . disarmed. She was under veils of color
plates. A different organ was painted on each—decoys. Which real

ones were missing? She allowed pain to circulate, lacking words for it.

Where was the water? One eye popped opened. Like a little fish. Panic declared itself. She was petrified. Pulsing. Palpable heat, heartbeat taking over for speech. Phrases floated to the surface, turned into music, drifted out to sea. Sounds were torn from her, and colors from the plates. She was giving birth to a bluebottle. Bleeding, leaking membrane. Shock first then flux. All falling down from her.

Set far back, black speck, heap, washed up on the beach. Head but no legs or scales—Hairy Tangled Ball. Maybe it wouldn't sting her. She looked it in the eye; it was all washed up. And Jane, who never cried, wept quarts.

***

"Terrible."

"Ghastly. I *told* you dear."

Jane was asleep, but she opened her eyes. Dick was standing next to the bed. By his side was a woman with short, curly hair, dressed in an unflattering pair of pine-green slacks and matching vest. Dick grasped a large bouquet of tiger lilies still in their pink wrapping.

"These are for you," he said, dropping them down on the bed.

Jane tried to turn toward the wall, but found she couldn't move her head.

"*Help* her," said the woman to Dick.

"No—don't."

Dick took a small step back and spoke rapidly. "This is dreadful . . . your neighbor told me . . . I went to your house . . . about the phone call . . . I, I wanted to apologize . . . it isn't something that happens everyday . . . I promise you it will *never* happen . . . well maybe not *never* . . ."

The woman elbowed Dick's arm. "I think she wants something," she whispered.

Jane was pressing on the nurse's signal.

'Well," Dick continued, "I wanted you to meet Sally, my . . . fiancée."

Sally slipped her hand into the crook of Dick's arm.

"I met Sally at the meeting . . . you know, the *group*. You must come, too—when you're better, of course."

Jane kept her thumb on the button.

"Is there anything we can do for you?" Sally asked.

Jane took a deep breath and croaked, "I don't want you to be here."

"She's tired, Dick."

Dick and Sally went away. Instead of the nurse, a lion came, to give Jane her pill. Jane slept.

Jane was awoken by a familiar voice. "Hey, how's about some Chinese food? You like Chinese? Yum yum. Lo mein noodles with those itty-bitty shrimps or maybe some steamed dumplings? Me, I could eat a elephant. You need to put some meat on those bandages of yours."

Jane lay motionless. It hadn't occurred to her to eat, though they'd already taken the IV out.

"What's that door there lead to? Hey get a load of this!"

Jane tried to lift herself out of bed. Her body was encased in a hard shell. She thought it might be possible to move slowly, one part at a time, but when she moved her right arm toward the edge of the bed, a jolt of pain shot up her side. Next she tried to move her legs. She felt a stabbing sensation all the way up her back. She lay down defeated.

"C'mon! Hit this one outta the park! Do it for the kid!"

Jane lifted her head an inch from the pillow. It must have weighed fifty pounds. When she tried to move the rest of her, she realized she was stuck to the bed. Summoning all her strength, she peeled herself bit by bit from the sheet. It was as if she were being flayed in reverse. She sat up and fastened her eyes on the door. There were gray and green specks all around her. Her head throbbed.

"Atta girl."

Her feet found the floor. She leaned on the lion's shoulder and hoisted herself up. They tottered through the glass door onto a balcony. The sun was setting. She had never been able to focus on long distances before. They must have done something to her eyes.

She looked up and smiled. There were no stars but she saw the blinking red taillights of planes as they descended into Queens. She glanced back over her shoulder at the bright room, expecting to see someone. No one appeared.

"It's good to be alone, huh?"

"You said it."

She rested a while on the balcony. It was cold but she was warm. She looked down at the parking lot full of cars. She watched a panel truck back carefully into a narrow space. She held her breath as it nudged its way in. Then she laughed and the lion laughed.

VICIOUS VICES OF EARLY LIFE

Asthma

Often she refuses, the room too cold. Always she eschews the fumes of oranges. Here was a faint woman with epaulets on her sweater. Others were sweltering while she took sultan raisins. She arranged herself mightily. The country was a place she had spoken of in tongues for she was afraid of bugs. Moths mainly. Before the lights could be turned out she must confront her demons. Surely hers was a plump reaction, lashing out like twins to pudding.

Gathering in the Head

She dug a hole to put her parents in. She used a ladle, a little dirt each day. Spade they took away from her. Hand trowel verboten. When they wrenched away the soupspoon she had tiny hands to tunnel down. At night the gardener filled the dimple in the earth. Later the sight of vines made her scream.

Parents Were Cousins

She loved Robert Louis Stevenson. She was a beauty but who knew it? He knew his father whoever he was would take him shooting. The moon was full, grass kissed her white feet. Helas enter chorus. No avail.

Grief

They made him drown the kittens in a sack. They threatened to take the piano away and they did. Indelible monochrome, ice cream dripping down his hand. He was his mother's favorite. A sensitive, musical child.

Sunstroke

Armand longed to cross the Sahara. *S'assoir dans le sable, sous les étoiles.* The soft rhythm of the camels, below hollow bowls of dune, oh oracular silence, enormous white light. In the panorama of another planet he saw animals, kept them off with fire. One night he burned his turban *par hasard.* They found him raving in the blazing sun.

Jealousy

Cashmere. Here was a man who was once a boy genius. Here was a man who liked boy geniuses. She was bad bad bad. He put his big foot on her. She liked a mess. Spilling was her game. He announced blithely they weren't blood related. She let it slip she was Rasputin's doppelganger. And so on.

Kicked in the Head by Horse

He lived at the bottom of a big hole in an orange mummy bag. He didn't look stupid. He lived on figs. She complained about his teeth—that's the way it was with her. I noticed his hands; they looked like smart hands to me. That hair, and those big blank black eyes, he looked to everybody including himself like a cockeyed Christ. He asked me to bring him back a tuna fish sandwich when he knew I was leaving for good.

Fear and Loss of Lawsuit

Money mattered, that much was clear. He chose to live without furniture. Chairs and tables were for idiots. He must, at all costs, never answer the phone or let on that he was home. He crept out at night to scout the papers for new developments. How content he would be to be seen in a café. How silly the affair seemed, but he would be vindicated, that much he believed.

Bad Company

Because they cannot see Alice doesn't mean she isn't there. She is exactly like the girl, only less mental. She has a more delicate palate, never mixes food with food, drinks only lemon water—as little as she can. The girl felt she herself was easy to please, but Alice was another story.

Intemperance

Aloxe-Corton he would serve with the fish or perhaps the safe Puligny-Montrachet. With the boeuf there would be ruby Chambertin, and the violet-scented Romanée-Conti. Meursault for the cheese. Then the simple Mirabelle, for it was just plain supper *d'un seul.*

Imaginary Female Troubles

First she thought it was cute the way he liked to dress up in her clothes. Then he stole her diary. Then her letters. And he was supposed to be some bloody great writer.

Doubt About Mother's Ancestors

As the session proceeded, a bluebird flew straight into the glass. "The same incident occurred when I consulted Herr Doktor Freud," she confessed. "Ein blau, blaue, blauen," he mumbled to himself, before reciting the segment of the dream she'd entirely forgotten. "You are rowing on a lake in the direction of Cluny. I must inform you, you were born there and I can assure you that, unless precautions are taken, you will certainly die within those same convent walls. At all costs, stay away from the Rhône—the oiseau clearly proves it. Trek east along the silk route to the Sayan Mountains; it is there where you will find solace."

Bad Whiskey

He played the crooked card game, wiped his ass with wanted dead or alive signs. She came to him in silk kimonos, unbidden. Didn't need no Doc Holliday to shoot him full o' holes.

Business Nerves

Large, barn-like structures, fundamental, but, in all respects, adequate, erected to house the elderly, infirm, and genetically inferior specimens, including artist populations. All equity will be accessible to, and channeled through, only those deemed deserving of it, having demonstrated their worthiness by means of their keen appreciation and abuse of power.

Women

"What do they want from us?"

1

All night everything was ending. Happiness defected to another family. "And how was your day," she would ask him. "Stupidly perfect. More like a gesture than a day," Karenin complained. The declension of bright start-overs divisible by a televised parade of swan-girls. "The more we want swift return, simulated union, apparel. . . ." He began talking at length about resurrection. "Another drawn-out expository with pointed indifference," she sighed. Her phlegmatic eyewear and his long-suffering cravat were at cross-purposes. It would be interesting to see where he stood when the universe broke in two.

2

"I think . . ." "Prunes, don't get started on that again." He felt he was above brand-name bifurcation. Fixatives like fidelity and flight spelled fiction in her book. Anna paused to sense the tremor of the planet, wobbling in its lopsided orbit. Or the pull of an older world with more accessories.

3

Death came like a door suddenly blown open by the wind. Then came the stationing of strangers taking polaroids. All at once she was a widow. She put on a disc. Schwanengesang always took away the bottom. Her problem was how to undo the domino of numbers. And redemption, threadcount, smog and plate tectonics all tossed together. Distilling dirt from money had driven some people mad (it was one of the paradoxes of modernism).

4

"Grizzled cult! Esthetes! Back away from the door!" The lamb showed up with pince-nez and a supercilious grin. He said his name was Andrey Bely, and he bore a striking resemblance to Andrey Bely.

"Where are your works on paper?" he demanded.

Movers took away the divan. "When she doesn't sing, she counts. When she stops counting, she sings. When she's not singing, she's counting. When she's not counting or singing, she cries," the factotum explained to the lamb.

"*Tu es vraiment dégueulasse.*"

Animal cruelty. Movie lies. Levin missing. The blank noise of lack.

"An excursion to the seashore could alter everything."

"Ah, peregrination . . . is just so sweet you want to disappear," Bely brayed leaving.

5

Her fertility was mental. After all who can fault the wind? Well, everyone. It wasn't like her to ask why. She was going to die. She put on another disc. An oblong monologue about herself or transport. Dwelling on events that may never have happened. In her mind's eye: Alma Ata. And dread of slipping through the tissue of the ridiculous. Listening to the adagio she felt as lonely as the moon, and fell asleep with her hands in her pockets

6

In the Bildungsroman, the hero never reads the gazette but deliberates his own demise or mankind's. She read *The Lives of the Saints*. At a moment's notice she could give up whom she desired. The paste of her saintly pallor. She ambled along yawning like a dog.

7

Would he call on her again, the lamby? She guessed *nyet* with certitude. He was the type who liked to stay up late and make senseless rhymes. That morning he offered her fish in a bucket if she could fetch him water without the bucket.

8

She spilled two glasses of tea but still had the keys to the dacha. At least the confiture and poesie were still intact. She had wanted him to stay all day, in the bathroom. She should have lacquered herself, put butter in the butter dish. "There goes the muse, the sepulchre, the tidy sacrifice, witless but uplifting reason," she thought as the door blew open.

"Cuttlefish! Why pay a fine for sugar! What are you, period. Nice and crisp, mind you!" Palimpsest, his calling card. "Anna?" Or was it palindrome?

"While you were away, I dreamt I was throwing everyone and breaking them, just like a child."

"Angels are allowed to watch but they can't get involved."

". . . trying to break the sound habit of reasoning."

"Yet since Vronsky you keep changing the subject back to yourself."

". . . to show up as myself in mimesis."

"Just imagine a devouring dragon in a crinoline. Medusa with more élan."

"That's your remedy for glossolalia?"

"Do you have any Pop-Tarts?"

"I have some lamb chops."

"Register your anguish as it breaks your heart and makes you want to die. Sign here."

This devochka must lie. "Diaries take up space," she thought.

"Everything is born in ether," she tried.

"It's Folsom for you this time baby," he replied.

Your basic enfant térrible. Behold, what, gone. "Goodnight sweet pike, goodnight, goodnight. . . ." Her toy-boat voice bobbed up and down over the surface of the song.

9

Or danger hanging voluptuously in mid-air, ebbing and flowing of faces, bedlam of incandescent limbs, vehicles, ragged archetypes, handy alchemical settings, lingual bridges to concomitant connectors, any system would do, certain death: sleeplessness.

10

Layered innuendo and memory. Checklist of her shortcomings. The poseurs were dropping like flies. The others were just lucky at cards. The next card she turned would bring her closer to death. There was the anesthesia plus the shiny lubricants they use for electroshock. Women from another continuum stood at the foot of her sledge. "Snap out of it, Anna."

(*To be concluded*)

THE POET-LIAR was it then? Tears in the appendix. She'd assembled a mental glossary of his likes, lapses, and an ardent cartography of his scars, marks and deep-seated phobias. Who else could love you? And the names came tripping off the tip like lemmings. Enter babbling courageous vanity dwarfing the muddled sibling, sloth. "Spittle on stigmata," she reminded herself, spreading saliva on the ripe sling-back sandal cuts, passion smoothie rumbling in her tummy.

I dreamed her up in a pink cocktail number now here she is. Bowls of green olive oil. Improbability of separating suggestion from death. She hadn't pictured the prince yet but he appeared on the scene all right slipper-bearing. "Will you . . . would you. . . ." Called away from the set by fairy-tale oblation. "You have taken off all your clothes," she rejoined. He exited left, lulled by dim glory, its stingy luster. A greedy leap to one-up them all.

In the beginning, stupor. Crocks of it. Blessed homilies. Not the cloying scent of his condescension, but the double-edged pendulum of conviction. Hate tantalizes. Like that alabaster bistro with the sign that used to say BAR but now says PREVARICATE. Or the blank shudder of an animal thinking, "What could I be thinking?"

There the light would be different. The tiny voice of abject terror in her bookmarking penitence. "Stop thinking," she said to herself. "Few have succeeded at that," answered a thought. "Count to ten and think about the fact there were no rats in Iceland until they were brought by ship." "Everyone knows in the director's cut

Dutchboy takes his finger out and gets crushed to death." The special effort not to bawl in aboreta. Rose wrapped in redfoil. In her mind's eye another city. Ambiguous still life. Transparency. Reversing the negative.

Was a camera necessary? He was in no hurry to leave the mirror. They were all over wanting to be all over one another. Lost to the condign. Dick floating in her dream, the tip of turnaround. The mind sets up perception without awareness. Hazy weather especially at the beach. Exited the set. Scruples intruding on the bassline.

Unbreathable atmosphere of her gloom. The sleepknot she tied inside herself, banging against it. Touch's sojourn on Elba. The swooping gift grafted to nostalgia. Tender headlong veiled ardor ripples. Would she send him view of annunciation on lagoon with cave moss decay? "Wish you were here. Banished. On this horned precipice. Crag of pure want. Room with unslept yearn. Cramped purple firmament comforting. Leprosarium. Galloping languor topped by gypsy-camp baptism. The stray blaze (inactive volcano). A day of sheer gauze. One snag: buried alive. Starkly, the heroine of clocks."

Silk whispers. Simple brow. Light exploring eyes, not her stalag search-lamps. Reticent petal, any psalm. The delicate link to silence, luminous redemption, adieu then, curtain slit, kimono sleeve. Eternal sleep.

"Where is the solemn plow, sentient and uncorrupted?"

"What smothers peril but politesse," she intuited. Notice the ferocious omens like elysium dong quai. Her netherworld *was* built in a day. It was her last card and she played it. Rupture.

THESE WERE THE WORDS

IT'S TRUE THAT I'm still alive but what does that matter. Clearly, one can live through anything, then die and go on living. I'd stopped considering the options. I was considering them all the time, cards I kept shuffling, entertaining asphyxia on the bus. I would lapse into Galician folktunes, but the prospect of war raging on the front changed nothing. I was the cause of the war—I alone. Cold comfort knowing my tribe was lost. I was an abacus whose beads clicked only radicals.

***

Rolling to the center of the book—notice how the scrolls are equally weighted—my prize falls out, a message made of fable and fact. By nightfall, the plagues are knocking at the door. Out in the street I'm lost. The signs have been taken down and the stores, except for the optical shop, have closed. Some are boarded up; in others I can see the same machines, shoes, and porcelain as before. The sky is unchanged though there's less of it. Where am I supposed to go? Are these the same names as before? I couldn't have been more than four. Turning the corner, I find myself in the forest. There is silence. I'd forgotten the sunset. Was that any of my business? And over the hilltop? I remembered that I'd forgotten how to *daven*.

***

The door was put back in place, first you, then I, took a turn closing it softly. Then I stepped over the threshold and went back to sleep though I was sleeping already. I'd second-guessed myself again, told myself to go on without me. In the dark, my bad luck began to dilate, just before my cue to walk into the ocean. My itchy kilt chafed my thighs. I tried to rub them across the wall. But the wall had fallen. And now there was nothing to stop the planets from skipping light, leaving home, going mad—no space for streets or for the mass graves that surfaced. Only the moon was left prowling in the senses. With each star a beholder.

***

The day ends violently with the flight of striped horses. In the officers' hall a round of slivovitz. I held the card that implied a journey, which only proved my house-on-fire tactics weren't cutting it. I remembered the brown-smelling garden; bored perennials that could only bloom. And I remembered the features of my last tender companion—Daddy Longlegs. Falling in with the image of poise. Repose? A gentle bell has no equal.

***

By the time summer rolled around, the charges were dismissed. He dropped by in his shorts with the vague pallor of the hunted. We got into some light slashing and senseless foreplay. Then he divided the wafers. "Where's that underwater bass solo coming from?"

"That's my stomach." "I wonder what magma's like?" "It's gotta be hotter than high school." Around three in the afternoon, I thought I heard Mr. Softee, but it was only some grave-tinsel vendors. "I guess we ought to get some studying done." I opened to the chapter, Epiphany: FAQs. "That's a gut course," he said, shutting the book. I looked into his eyes; it was one of those song moments. Then the cloud of equanimity passed over and, as usual, my earth depravity was nullified.

***

She said everything she thought to everybody always. "Au revoir," when she left, though there'd be no meeting again. We spent a long time talking about the nature of evil. We agreed evil is something that cannot be reasoned with. Later I came to see that evil was nothing special. I looked through the notebooks that recorded her thoughts. "I am not a person with whom it is advisable to link one's fate." She had a bone to pick with purity. She had hoped one day to become a vagabond, or to have a life in which there was no room for choice. Affliction was the means of her salvation that never let her forget the cause of her *malheur* which was self-inflicted.

***

We open deep inside the mine inside the mind. A box suspended in the air. Actually bolted to the edifice abutting it, and everything inside the box was bolted down but could be easily removed with a claw. Objects were preferable to façades but movable objects were disallowed. The clocks made no sound. The steady, heavy thud came from . . . we never found out. We never even knew how we got here. There were several doors. Behind any one of them, cold, smooth surfaces jutted out from the wall. Seamless darkness extended from the threshold. Another door maybe miles ahead. Proceeding by touch or crawling on the floor toward the stillness that didn't belong to space. Everything I knew was wrong. A fall would do me no harm. I was someone who wished she'd never seen the light of day.

***

She was trying to make an appointment with an important man. "Is your schedule flexible?" he asked. "Very flexible." She had all the time in the world. He had a light, gracious manner. She breathed into the phone. He said, "No, I'm sorry, I don't have any time at all." "Neither do I." "Let's meet at the fountain in the Plaza." "I'll be wearing a blue cockade in my chapeau." "And I'll be festooned in clupeids." "I can't stand a fishy smell." "Wouldn't you know it . . ." "What are you saying?" "And my chiffonier is just being delivered." "My gecko is having a panic attack." "I'm only in the city seven minutes a week." "I've got to fax my animus." "I'll pencil you in for Saturday." "I know a great place to bury bones." "Maybe we could squeeze in a talkie." "I wanted to ask you something—do you believe in ghosts?" "Yes, I'm a bachelor." "You know, I can't read music." "That's all right. I know a certain pilot." "Near Dijon?" "Not even close."

***

I had no scarf but shouldn't have needed one. Mockery hadn't entered my mind. Wrongs rattled in me—smugness notably, not a blessing. "'When a good man dies, his soul becomes a word and lives in God's book.' Some guy said that." His trousers were too long and too short. Bowed down, back rounded, his chin held up, even as his head drooped, not drooling yet. I was losing. I couldn't give up the gloom—my refusal, or fatigue, a sharp ache around the collarbone. For the moment I had no complaints. My eyes were growing used to the dark; it was easy to believe I owned the sun. He began to outline piety, its essential features, not just rites but a personal touch. "This isn't the time to throw light my way." But I wasn't running. Nearness of sanity crept up like reverence. I knew I wasn't supposed to look at the moon, but there it was waxing and waning. What could be overlooked? Personality? I began by tearing it down, and later, a little further on, building it back up. A fragile silence, labored breath. I was beginning to get tired, and I let my eyes close. Yearning started in me and ended somewhere else. In the absence of a scarf, it was easy to see what was needed most.

***

Mother came to me in dreams. I locked her out of my day thoughts. I had come to expect her in the last four minutes before waking, a hand reaching up from opaque water to pull me under and scold me. I meant to write it down but was lulled into forgetting. It's been years since I've been able to look in the mirror. The body is of no consequence. And the dress? Dressing up for poverty got me nowhere. No one could explain why my shoes were nailed to a board. The last excursion was from the mirror through the labyrinth, with the thread concealed. Where were the simple words meaning themselves? Or actual things needing no words? What I heard were the sounds preceding birth and following death, though I couldn't prove it.

***

For one thing, I didn't speak the language. Through the window the river reflected the blinking sign. I found one area scarcely distinguishable from another. Further along the bank I heard twigs and trash crackling in a burning cistern. I took out my buttons and counted, sitting in the armchair, dressed compliantly for supper, box balanced on my knees. The room went from dull to dim in a minute. My eyes closed. Normally, I get up and turn on the gas. Then I inspect the stove, the total situation. The deeper memory, or murmur, at dusk. A ghost? It's her again. Playing tricks with the sky. Understanding is a slow process. These were the words but not the names. It is not enough to understand the words; what's necessary is to reply.

***

I'd been invited to join the colony again, but once there I knew I'd be excluded. Nevertheless my bags were packed. I was a direct descendent of Pocahontas and couldn't help flaunting my test scores. I had no connection to convenience and was proud of my galoshes. I fingered my passport which smelled like milk. On no account would I renew it. Once I got there, I didn't work every day. I had no excuses. I would hide behind the greenhouse, near the furze, for hours. When it rained, I stayed inside the main estate with a puzzle; then the clinic became a second home. They examined my head and my heart, with negative results. I managed to locate a birthday cake I had baked myself and found some plain happiness.

***

She hadn't associated girls with happiness. Growing up among refugees had done that. But so what? Wasn't it still possible to get free meals in a foreign land. She didn't fit in with the druids. They had told her to leave for good, but stay in touch. Anyway, the real news was someplace else. Two years ago she'd been at the top of her game. Nothing had changed, except the trains were late and later everything was late. She didn't want to emigrate. But at least *he* was in the city—the wrong one. She confined herself to political intrigue. News from the Terminus, how many roundups? Idly wondering whether to change history one way or another. Could an act of faith do that? She was content to lie in the cellar, next to the big wine barrels. Finally, she wasn't considered important enough to interrogate. Any impending uprising was crushed in the cradle. She slept with the light on, tied to a bedpost until they came to wake her. She expected to be extradited any day but wasn't. This was the kind of anti-climax she was getting used to.

***

He was stuck back there behind the wall. Of course there was no wall anymore. I advised him to open a restaurant that featured polenta dishes as a concession to the Carpathians, paprika for the Hungarians, tapioca for the Brazilians. He wrote that he'd sold his bicycle and I felt a wave of melancholy and resentment. It would not be possible to get rid of him after all. He was like a dog. There was some intelligence, but I had stopped trying. I thought of myself as coming from a well-to-do family; I had an active correspondence with parents whom I'd dreamed into existence. "Let me know who's to blame for the executions and whether you'll be attending the wedding. Perhaps it's really no one's fault." But the sheep kept me from getting even as far as the verandah. "Instead of slaughtering them, I'm going to teach them Midrash." How I could stay in the soup for so long was by simply not telling anyone about it. I had no cause to fear the opposite sex. Only here was an occasion to reinvent sacrifice.

***

Once I started on my pilgrimage, I couldn't stop. I didn't like the way the twigs felt on my face. I couldn't have been more than four. Tramping along in the dust, I'd refused a spoken language—cuneiform was good enough. I wouldn't disclose what would have been wasted in speech. I stopped to rest or sleep or make suggestions by hand signals. Usually they condemned me. A brown cloud was my steadfast companion. I saw the canal in a vision and described it to anyone who would listen, but they kept cutting me off with their own versions. As twilight fell, I changed direction. As if I were dreaming my way to rain. Geography was a thief of eleven miles a day. Singing as the numbers flew from my head. Three or four paces north, a downpour. Sinking my keepsakes in the mud, squinting at the sun. My goat was dead. Seven years I wandered in the desert. Over one hill, I saw the canal. There was some emotion.

***

They told me there was crud stuck to the strawberries, that the peaches would never ripen. According to them good news is ruin. It was not worthwhile to be a woman. They said they could do a much better job. In my handbag paper wings were neatly folded. They found my questions about things left behind hard to swallow. It was against the law to count. I prayed not to, not to see again. But I saw them again in the dust. Demolition crews were knocking through the orphanage wall. I didn't know I'd been stricken from the town records.

***

The general appearance of the clouds, and the smokiness of the camp hadn't changed. The horses had tired faces and empty carriages were circled like wagons in a western. I lifted the jug, cradling it in the crook of my arm, surprised to find some whisky at the bottom. Bells again. This time I wouldn't make the mistake of believing. I remembered the pebble levy at the end of the path. But where was the path? Were these the same crackers left over from lunch? Apart from the abstract wall just above the water was the reflection of a statue of a nameless saint. The blackbirds did their best to make me feel welcome, bringing me clumps of straw in their beaks. But the scales were tipping. For the rest of the day there was intermittent screeching. I didn't struggle. I kept another jug under the porch steps. My impulse was to fill it with straw—probably not the right thing to do. Have I learned my lesson—any lesson? I would have liked some buttercups. That would have ended it nicely. What good would the word for "blackboard" do me?

***

I lingered over the shell game, rooted to the prospects. The probability of exile or return. All roads did not lead back to me. One day I was visited by two men. They debated what I was. She's more than a weasel, one of them said. They made me an offer. I accepted their handshakes. Slick unguent stuck to my hand. It was the smell of almonds that awakened me. Or menace lurking in me. I heard and saw but did not understand. My inclination was to conceal words but they were desperately needed to fulfill the promise of prayer.

***

I was only living in order to die. When I sang a song the Cossacks beat me. If you counted you'd be short or have too many. I lived in order to ruin my life. There were few wounds, several errors. Sent by the dead who lived in the corners. I couldn't find what I was looking for, knew it didn't exist. Soon the moon slipped away. I was sleeping in an open pit. I'd never been kissed. Suddenly I was forced to do what I was unable to do.

CORTON-BRESSANDES. Where had I gotten it and when? Years had elapsed. I thought of very hard limestone. Subsoil lava. "It's the end of suffering," he iterated, handing me the tumbler. Raw and gamey—grimy even. Finesseless compared to its Côte d'Or cousins. I tasted truffles plus any number of alluvial accidents. Then I was dead.

Crevice. A wall, vortex, tremendous push-through, not the New Age winnowing you see on Death TV. At the end, the cordial sluice. Then the tearoom: dirty cups, anodynes, or the cure for talking. The Blenginy texture of cerements, migratory tatters, scrappy orphans' moulderingwear, persistent woolens, passionflowers withered, everlasting seamstresses' brocade created by the naked spade. My invisible mouth blossoms in air, proof of breath, bandaged.

Some brittle apparition of "home," this ebony scheme. Boneyard stones with those dimestore seraphim were in my book sweeter than Bellini. "Exhort Poor Booty Trinket Snow Blank Bliss." Bored, I took a tour of druidical home décor, frilly ossuaries. Artful sepulchres full of ornament and dreck, cobwebbed cherubim, concrete sarcophagi. A shrill vermilion galaxy of agony. Plank dominion's call—blind embarrassments—painted rose under the lid, heft of posthum contraband, "tenant on earth," ignominy's babble, calvary, crucifixion. To tell the truth, spool, slotted spoon, petticoat, rain, echo—not eternity, spectacles, misery, train whistle—was where the soul resided.

Passing on to poor lighting, the smells that are like a whisper. An underwater Chartres with pillars but no vaults, and spooks dressed to the nines. I hadn't the clothes for anything unheimlich. Only my age remained the same, not my shadow. Loose-fitting gown of my departure barely noted.

I tried to talk but the habit had left me. Unheard, I scribbled hastily in the air. I had to give up my shoes if I expected to get anywhere. Had I learned to love the High Holy Days? Slowly then the lights came up. I crawled out of brightness into nothing.

I BOUGHT TINY octopi in season to please him. And I had only just struck up a conversation at the gravlax counter. But how many men do you meet these days who can trace their bloodlines back to Copernicus? In his eyes I saw the steady decline of a very old world where mauve and brevity really stood for something.

We stopped on Orchard Street for mun danish. I bought underpants with phases of the moon. Then he rode me home on his Harley, but the poppyseeds left us so addlepated we veered off the FDR into the river. Not an auspicious beginning. We agreed to meet again for drinks—at my place, since he was dead. Anyway, I was just as glad to get back to the story I was writing.

At the time I was living in an abandoned train terminal off Twelfth Avenue. Dark mission oak and WPA art made it night all the time which was no problem. Beauty makes me jumpy but I love clutter. Who doesn't like to find a Kewpie in the heap or a bulb horn á là Harpo. Books crumbled to dust. Many empty samplers; mementos' lonely chorus, ". . . because you're the only good thing that ever happened to me."

Searching for what—pancakes?—yet it was hard to find a single soul who could construe "short stack." I was like a broken compass needle spinning where the saints had vacated.

Call it a pilgrimage. You may not believe it when I say I've never *been* to Romania. "You'll never come back," the matron at the passport office told me. "I will buy a coat there," I said to her. I wasn't thinking about Bucharest but about love. Leaving for the airport immediately, I brought with me my unseeded rye. I didn't have time to read every book in the library.

Shouting and general commotion among the passengers as we touched down at Timiçoara. Potent plum spirits were passed around in a sheep-stomach flask. An old woman stood up in the aisle and began reciting verse about saxifrage. I felt a surge of Danubian nostalgia for terrain wholly unknown to me. I couldn't tell saxifrage from savory, yet when I heard the words said aloud in Rumanian I swear that I could smell it. I could see the inside of the Poienari Castle. I knew where the scepters were kept and the potions to make one fall in love or die writhing. I inquired about trains to Sighisoara. It was great to be back in medieval Europe.

Had I boarded the wrong train or overslept and missed my connection? "Tee karranteen?" demands the conductor nudging me from slumber. A boy anywhere from eleven to seventeen as pale as daikon translates, "You quarantine?" Heads swaddled in rags, the sharp smell of disinfectant. I cover my mouth with the serviette the conductor rents me for seventy rubles—hepatitis B&C, cholera, diphtheria and undulant fever are close and ready.

Vistas of bleak desolation. Hospital, housing block, airport—abandoned, plundered, rotted, forgotten. The dream of a new regime radio waves no longer reach. Had Kazaks once wandered here? Ghostly nomads roaming the steppes. We pass the atomic lake—konechnaya, "the end." The train jolts to a stop in the desert. We are forced to debark.

Crouching for shade under the train, I spy tarantula families. Coming my way at goodly speed, a five-foot prehistoric monitor. "Don't let them put anything in your pockets," whispers a woman I hadn't seen before, in near-perfect English. I notice she looks a great deal like me. But she is a man. Am I a man, too?

After they fix the "refrigerator," we all get back on the train, except for the sick and elderly, who are left outside to die. I see the boy who'd translated earlier already dead there. The train rolls on. We turn sharply north, toward the death camp in the tundra. Out of my valise spill smelly syringes, any one of which could neutralize me instantly.

Thus ends the first day of my vacation.

NO PLAY

HINDSIGHT SUBJUGATION. An infinity of fallopian trappings, togs for baby goats, lots of loot, a pail to load it in. Card-shark applicants bring with you two to four fags, an old waxy crayon, soft boots, a damp napkin. Know our top brass may occasionally sanction rubbing duck fat on your skin. Fractious boas molt prior to arrival. Unconscious coiling, as you know, is a flagrantly malicious ritual. Honor our animal libido by ssssing or biting sporadically.

Thanks for your continuing succor. Blini and umbilical insults will accompany awful singing in our main lobby. Stroll at random, shallow and rapacious, visit our gift shop or buy wool shawls with flaws knit by antsy nuns. Nihilists and panophobics you may stay in your rooms all day and rot. Philosophical inquiry, conundrum, quibbling or quandary about living and/or dying, including any koan, is off limits in dining halls A–Z. Kick our staff viciously on a whim —that's what our boys and girls long for. If you kill your maid or pool guard, that's okay. Many of our poor local lads want crappy jobs that pay squat.

Sanguinary boars, stubborn swans, and lazy platypi must pick a juicy ditch to swill and swash in. Odor is bad, as is candor. Bankruptcy is good but hardship and privation bad. Disdain is good, without passion. Stick to our fatuous 4H chant: Hunting, Having, Hoarding, Hubris. Fuck humanity. Cling to fuzzy infractions of charity—wow. Vacuous wags bask in bland casuistry. Sycophants wassail insipidly. Gorgons, this is your day.

WHAT COLOR ARE YOUR UNDERPANTS?

WHAT COLOR UNDERPANTS are you wearing? Ordinarily, I am the kind of person who likes to keep things to herself. I like to keep changing the story, remembering different things, inventing them or moving them around. I like thinking about a particular moment over a period of days, what I'd forgotten, a statement, a simple gesture, a silence or a pause, something that wasn't supposed to happen, or something that happened as anticipated. I tell the story about myself, or try to figure out how it might appear to someone outside the story, or try to grasp the bigger picture, a bird's-eye view of the main events. Often I continue the story from where it ended, what I predict will come to pass, with entirely plausible or fantastic events, so that a prospective visit to meet someone's family will turn out to be an interrogation by the secret police. I try to keep the story going for as long as I can, layering all the versions, comparing and/or conflating them, reflecting on what's changed—what might have been, had something else happened, had I done something else or known what I know now—thinking of these things, long after they took place. Others are often surprised when I bring to mind things they can never recall; there are times, too, when I want to forget some of these things though it seems to me they've only just occurred.

Naturally this has little to do with what's happened, as it hadn't "happened." In general, I'm reluctant to talk about personal encounters, especially as they are happening. Usually I can tell how something will turn out, as if it weren't happening to me, in the same way one is unable to stop watching a movie even though the outcome is known in advance.

There were times, though, when I wasn't able to guess what would come next. Because I was home, inside my apartment, it seemed like nothing could happen to me. I had stopped seeing Y. We weren't living together. It took me a long time to not think about it. I became impatient to get over it. I didn't feel like going out. What I felt was that my life with Y. was still going on, only without him. I pretended to be open to new experiences. It wasn't exactly a break from him, more like a weekend vacation.

I wondered, too, if I could do it. I told myself this was only a drill. You like it when I watch, don't you? he said. You have a German name, I said. He said, I like make-believe. So did Y. What do *you* think of it? I replied that I wasn't sure, though I *was* sure. I told him I thought it was fun. He wanted to know what I look like, what size my breasts are, and not knowing what to answer, I give him a short description and the number thirty-two. He asked me what I like and I mentioned some things I'd done or imagined. I said I wouldn't mind trying something new. I think simple is best, he said, and I agreed, but what was "simple?" I wasn't sure. Was simple hypothetical? He wasn't tied to extravagant plots and ploys. That's what I thought he meant by simple. He asked me if I liked animals and I said I did which was only partly true because I haven't played with imaginary animals since I was at university.

How do you like it here? he asked. I'm not afraid at all, I said, even though I'm a stranger and I can't speak the language. Is language so important? he asked. Yes, I said, the city is anonymous, but it's also familiar. I think I know this problem, he replied, it's when I return from the countryside back to the city. How do you feel then? I asked. Lost. I call up my friends——it takes a bit of time to adjust. But we're here and we're there, I said, we're both in the story. Yes, that's true, he agreed, and then there was silence. I touched a key and the room went dark. I lay in the dark awhile. Later I got up and went to the kitchen to make a cup of tea. I sat there for a time and thought about Y. and his work at the university on *Tinea pellionella*.

FURTHER ADVENTURES IN POETRY:

John Ashbery—*100 Multiple-Choice Questions*
Clark Coolidge—*Far Out West*
Chris Edgar—*At Port Royal*
Merrill Gilfillan—*The Seasons*
John Godfrey—*Private Lemonade*
Charles North—*The Nearness of the Way You Look Tonight*
David Perry—*Range Finder*
Jacqueline Waters—*A Minute Without Danger*

www.adventuresinpoetry.com